Writing Your Rhythm

Writing Your Rhythm
Using Nature, Culture, Form and Myth

Diane Thiel

Story Line Press, Ashland, Oregon

First Printing

Published by Story Line Press, Three Oaks Farm, PO Box 1240, Ashland, OR 97520-0055

This publication was made possible thanks in part to the generous support of the Nicholas Roerich Museum, the Andrew W. Mellon Foundation, and our individual contributors.

Book design by Lysa McDowell

Library of Congress Cataloging-in-Publication Data

Thiel, Diane, 1967–
     Writing your rhythm : using nature, culture, form and myth/by Diane Thiel.
       p.cm.
     ISBN 1-58654-006-8
     1. English language—Rhetoric—Problems, exercises, etc. 2.
     Poetry—Authorship—Problems, exercises, etc. 3. Creative writing—
     Problems, exercises, etc. I. Title

     PE1413 .T45 2001
     808'.042—dc21   2001049534

O swallows, swallows, poems are not
The point. Finding again the world,
That is the point.

— Howard Nemerov

The plants would grow there like the story,
strong and translucent as the stars.

— Leslie Marmon Silko

For my mother
and the generations of teachers
in my family

Contents

Writing from Culture / 87

Writing with Form / 127

Storytelling and Myth-Making / 213

Acknowledgments / 245

Introduction

You want to write. You may be wondering how to get started, or you may be seeking ideas to get yourself going again, or you may want to keep the momentum. There are over two hundred exercises in this book to help you discover ways to spark your mind, access your memory, record your thoughts, refine your language, and find your rhythm. In writing workshops, students sometimes call these exercises my "bag of tricks." True art, of course, is more than just "tricks" or "exercise." It arises out of the greatest extremes of our existence, and its source remains on some level mysterious. It is something which truly cannot be taught, something we must often stumble upon on our own. But the suggestions which follow will point out different paths you might follow. And the exercises will get you in shape, or keep you in shape, for when the stories and poems come in search of you.

The discussions and exercises in the book work for a variety of age ranges and backgrounds. There are examples, suggestions of additional models, and thoughts on writing from classical and contemporary writers of different cultures to emphasize the importance of lineage and influence. We learn by example, by emulation of elements of our cultural as well as our natural world. One of the best ways to develop your writing is to read widely and to model your favorite writers. I have also included responses from children and adults I have worked with to show the possible results of these exercises. Some exercises address specific works of literature, so they might provide insights in understanding and responding to these texts. They will also likely inspire ways to respond to other texts as well. Although some chapters work best in the arranged sequence, for the most part, feel free to move around, to leaf through and happen on a subject which intrigues you. The book offers exercises and examples to address the basics of writing, as well as innovative new approaches and connections. Some of the chapters have "links" to other sections noted, so you might travel through the book that way. The exercises could also be combined. You might use one from *Writing from Nature* and one from *Writing with Form*, for instance, to create a single piece. Although the book contains more examples of poetry (because of its relative brevity and the necessity of examples to teach poetic form), many of the exercises can be employed to generate either poetry or prose. And even working in different poetic forms will help to train your ear and have an influence on the rhythm in your free verse and prose as well.

I have long incorporated techniques of poetry to teach prose. For over ten years, I have been teaching creative writing in several programs—classes at Brown University, Florida International University, and University of Miami; an inter-disciplinary National Science Foundation program on Ecology for Urban Students; the Miami Book Fair's "Poet in the Schools" program; and workshops for teachers. My workshops often focus on the way writing poetry is useful to developing other writing as well. Poetry demands close attention to word choice, rhythm, figurative language, etc. Good prose, of course, must also have a regard for these elements. William Faulkner once quipped, "all novelists are failed poets." Rather than disparaging novelists, Faulkner was acknowledging the poetry at the root of all writing.

One intention of this book is to break down (or at least relax) our more recent societal distinctions—to access our lineage of poetry as story, as drama, as history, as science, even math. Pythagoras, in his search for the deeper meanings of numbers, was as much a mystic and poet as he was a mathematician.

I remember a conversation I had with Modesta, an Emberá woman I met on a recent trip to Colombia. She told me about the way the children in her tribe were educated. They learned their biology, physics, math, art, ethics, and stories in the forest, often in a single lesson. "You can learn everything from the forest," she said. I answered her with a comment about how education in my world, unfortunately, is compartmentalized according to subject, and takes place in small, separate indoor classrooms. At least I meant to say classrooms. Mid-sentence, I forgot the proper Spanish word and said *"cajitas"* instead, which is the word for "little boxes." But Modesta nodded, understanding completely.

The five sections of *Writing Your Rhythm time and space, nature: culture, form, and myth-making* overlap in many ways. We cannot address culture or myth without realizing that we are part of a whole, one which contains the same patterns repeated on both the largest and most infinitesimal scales.

I have worked for many years with first-year college students and have conducted workshops with many people who don't consider themselves "writers," who often initially approach storytelling or poetry with an attitude of "what's the point," or "why bother?" So this is one of the concerns we first address. Robert Frost, in an essay, "Education by Poetry," addresses this question, by suggesting that poetry plays an important role in the development of thinking. He discusses the importance of analogy in reasoning and emphasizes the power of metaphor, how we learn to link one thing to another. This kind of association challenges our minds and builds associative muscles. It also has the potential of unlocking the specialized boxes of society. Stories, too, have a far more powerful role in our lives than we may consciously recognize. We use them daily for such purposes as exchanging advice, teaching life's lessons, making community, and drawing connections between things. Leslie Marmon Silko opens her book *Ceremony* with the notion of story as ritual, as an organic part of her Laguna Pueblo oral tradition. "You don't have anything if you don't have the stories," she says.

One of the first assignments I give students in my workshops is to write about their relationship to writing, to use a metaphor to connect it to something else. In doing so, I often reconsider my own relationship. My definitions change or wear different faces. But the one thing always remaining constant is the tension which exists. On the one hand, we need the free run of the mind to generate ideas. On the other, a structure is necessary. It is like the tension we witness in the natural world. Louis Simpson has his memorable ars poetica, "American Poetry," which speaks to that tension, the balance between beauty and ugliness, nature and culture, form and freedom, specificity and universality:

> Whatever it is, it must have
> A stomach that can digest
> Rubber, coal, uranium, moons, poems.
>
> Like the shark, it contains a shoe.
> It must swim for miles through the desert
> Uttering cries that are almost human.
> —Louis Simpson (b. 1923)

Writing is a physical act, an extension of the body—in the act of creating, and in the act of reading or reciting. We become more aware of the potency and rhythm of words when we say them aloud. We inhabit them differently. "Poetry is made of words, not ideas," Mallarmé said to Degas, asserting his definition of poetry as being based on sound. There is a visceral pleasure inherent in reading, hearing, or reciting a poem with attention to form, in particular. Our bodies and minds respond to meter and rhyme. Working with children and experiencing their innocent physicality can remind us of this. One can tell what kind of language they like by the way their bodies dance to it. And our bodies themselves remind us of nature's incredible balance, the form which makes us function. Any breath might remind us, if we pay attention.

A pervasive theme in my workshops is to recognize the form we see in nature. In questionnaires I give at the beginning of workshops, invariably, most students hardly know anything about form in writing, but say that they want to be "free," that they want writing to be a "natural" process. And I do think that structure must be organic, that it should meet its subject at the crossroads. Writing is, in fact, a crossroads—a synthesis of varied elements. It is created out of the tension between form and subject.

The environments we inhabit might very well influence our sense of form. Both the form and the harsh subject matter of the work of Robinson Jeffers, for instance, was influenced by the rocky, unsheltered, and then undeveloped Carmel coast where he made his home. His long lines mirror the rhythms of the dramatic Pacific tides.

Goethe saw a great link between art and nature, particularly on the basis of three principles: "polarity" (the charge of opposites), "metamorphosis" (growth and change), and "heightening" (an intensification of the progressive change). But he believed that great art, though illuminated by nature, should transcend it and fulfill our instinctive desire for beauty.

Frederick Turner, in his essay "The Neural Lyre," in *Natural Classicism: Essays on Literature and Science*, suggests that when the left brain communicates with the right brain in writing, particularly with metrical variation, we develop our notions of time, improve our memory, and promote physical and sociological harmony. We reinforce a desire to make sense of the world in terms of beauty and goodness. This assertion based on human physiology certainly takes Frost's notion of education by poetry quite a step further.

The stories and history of cultures were passed down in poetry via meter and rhyme, useful as tools to enhance our memory. When we speak of the oral tradition, we often think of times as distant as ancient Greece, of Homeric songs carried from one place to another by memory. Modern Greece, however, is a good example of a place where the oral tradition has survived—perhaps because for many centuries Greece was under foreign rule. Writing could be censored, but no one could suppress or confiscate songs. There is a subversive quality to the oral tradition. One of Greece's best known contemporary poets, Yannis Ritsos, spent five years (1948-1953) in prison in the aftermath of the Greek Civil War because of his leftist politics. He continued to write poems and would bury them in bottles to hide them from the guards, but the only way he could get them to the general populace was in the minds of freed prisoners. They learned the poems by heart and smuggled them out.

Likewise, the tradition of blues poetry in this country arose partly out of the field songs of slaves, who often passed messages about the Underground Railroad via the call and response of their lines. With the many writers forcibly silenced or exiled from societies over the course of history, we have a sense of the subversive power that words can have in a culture—to awaken, challenge, move us to action. We understand why they were often feared by those in power.

But in our culture, does literature belong to the people? Do we feel like our stories and poems have power? Perhaps a reawakening of the oral tradition (storytelling and learning poems by heart) is one way to access the potency of our ancient and modern myths. It is also a way to re-connect with our natural world—to recognize and re-align ourselves with its patterns and rhythms. Writing, like music, is about juxtaposition, tension, and balance—principles we also find in the natural world. In their songs, for instance, whales sing the same lines to each other and vary them slightly as they travel. They employ a kind of meter and rhyme in their exchange. Granted, there are few of us lucky enough to have heard unrecorded whale song, but such examples of natural form are all around us, the intricate repeated patterns of sound and matter, of light and language.

Time and Space:
Getting Started

This section offers suggestions for finding the time and space for your creativity, as well as some means of accessing your memory. It also presents insights and exercises which address some of the basic foundations of writing.

Loosing the Flood

In every culture, there is a flood story, from Mesopotamia, to Greece, to the Mayan Popul Vuh. We often think of floods as purely destructive, but they are also restorative. They clear the way for new growth. Sometimes, we have to write just to find out what is going through our minds, to see it appear on paper. We write to find out who we are.

Free-writing is a way to catch that flood as it emerges. We have all had the experience of the perfect idea lost to the winds of the traveling mind, or the dream we desperately wished we could remember.

A journal is essential—a place to catch those ideas, to get them down on paper. Once they are there, you can worry about shaping them later. You might keep one journal, or several: a dream journal, a journal for class, a relationship journal. Thoreau kept separate journals for science and for poetry, but he admitted that science and poetry became extensions of each other for him, and he found it increasingly difficult to keep his observations separate.

Often, ideas arrive as gifts from the world around us. I was teaching a workshop one day, and students were doing a free-writing exercise. We had just been discussing how the writer will create a setting to reveal something about the internal struggle: like a heat wave linked to fierce agitation. As they began writing, the skies suddenly opened up, and a torrent poured down. We joked about the rain being a "physical manifestation" of the creative process in the room. We often use such serendipitous gifts: the thunderclaps at precisely the right moments. Or the gifts might belong to the more urbane world: One day, a student looking for a psychology project stuck his head in the room and asked, "Is this a class or an experiment?"

Nearly all of us, at one time or another, have flooded our friends with our troubles. The process is cleansing, rejuvenating, healthy. But it's a good idea to get a journal to catch some of the flood, so you don't drive your friends crazy. And you can save that material for later. Writing is a transforming experience, a place to turn the negative into the positive. Just put your pen to paper, and find out what is occupying your mind. We need to experience things before we shape them into writing, just as we usually need to experience the words on the page before we determine a form.

It can be a good idea to write by hand. Your writing will go through plenty of versions in the typed form, but try getting started with your pen to paper. Though the pen is becoming archaic in our world, there is something about forming words on the page that is decidedly physical.

Then, be prepared to "throw away" ninety-five percent of your writing (or rather, let it go no further than your journal). Realize that you will often write ten lines to get a single good one. Think of the journal as a no-pressure situation. There is never a "blank page" to face because your hand keeps moving.

Don't expect to emerge with a final piece right away. Writers often walk around with an idea for many years—a great idea that hasn't quite found its form, or its connecting force. Free-writing can help us find these connections, as we record the ebb and flow of our thoughts.

* * *

- Free-write for a set amount of time each day or several times a week.

- If you feel completely blocked, you might try this: play word association with yourself. Write down five words, the first words that come to mind. Any words. As I write this, I'm thinking of *photograph, father, newspaper, couch, tea.* One, or a combination of those words will create a host of associations and propel you forward.

- Try "writing" (or at least starting) a piece in the shower (I'm serious). Some of my best epigrams or first lines or combinations of words have arrived in the shower. It must be the flow of water. It has helped me exercise my memory over the years, because I had to devise some way to remember my ideas, or they would surely be lost. Jot down your thoughts as soon as you can.

- Start with the words "I remember..." Go with your first impulse. What memory is brimming?

- "Remember" something which you could not possibly remember, at least not according to a linear view of the world, as Creek poet Joy Harjo does in "Remember":

> Remember the moon, know who she is. I met her
> in a bar once in Iowa City...
> Remember the wind...I heard her singing Kiowa war
> dance songs at the corner of Fourth and Central once.
> —Joy Harjo (b. 1951)

The following example from a nine-year old-student contains many abstract words (I usually encourage students to make these more concrete; see *How You Say a Thing*). But the abstract words do seem to work here:

> I remember when the earth was small.
> I remember when there was nothing at all.
> There was blackness and darkness.
> There was coldness and hardness.
> I remember it all.
> —Jannis Brea, 4th grade

The Skeletons in Our Stories

Free-writing is useful for more than merely getting the ideas down on a page. Often, it helps a structure begin to emerge. Take an entry from your journal and see if there are patterns within. Do you notice a particular rhythm, repetitions, refrains? Does it want to be prose or poetry? A sonnet, a short story, a narrative poem? What is the tone? Is it angry, sad, pensive, humorous? There is much we can see in that initial surge to suggest what form the piece might take. We find our voices, our natural rhythms, perhaps the shape of a story to be told. We might have an idea about the form beforehand, but more often, the process is organic. And sometimes, in free-writing, we find ourselves finding a natural closure as we run out of time. The mind wants to return to the original leap.

The skeletons (or framework) of our poems, stories, and essays are what hold them together, and yet can often go virtually unnoticed by the average reader. Paying close attention to even the smallest components of a piece of writing, such as a creative use of grammar, can be a useful exercise for your own work. (See *The Grammar of the Situation* and *Parallel Lines*.)

Occasionally, good writing leaps fully formed from your head. But that is rare. So don't be lazy. Training yourself in such basics as meter and grammar will give your writing, both prose and poetry, an attention to structure and rhythm. (See *Writing with Form*.) You will also begin to recognize the great variety of forms which your writing can take. For instance, for a long time, I wanted to write about a childhood presentation I had done of Dante's *Inferno*. It appeared as "ideas" in several of my free-writes before it found its form—a narrative poem in loose terza rima, in "homage" to Dante's form in the work. (See *Old Myth, New Myth*.)

A major element of good writing is the ability to select the details that resonate, the ones that are specific enough, but also general enough to create that moment of recognition, or "fine remembrance," as Yeats terms it. Less is often more in writing. As you initiate the act of selection, the form of your piece might also begin to reveal itself, in draft after draft.

We sometimes have ideas that feel too huge to handle. First attempts may reveal the seeds of many different stories within a single piece. Beginning writers, in particular, need to be wary of letting their ideas harden or freeze into forms too quickly. After a first attempt, see if you can identify different entities emerging. You might focus on one voice, one component, one character's story at a time, perhaps, that will work towards a larger whole. Poetry helps us train for this, as poetry requires attention to the line, the foot, the right word. Occasionally, although a detail seems out of place in a story or poem, it feels too vivid or interesting to discard. It helps to think of such a detail as the seed of another piece. Sometimes, collections of related stories or poems grow via this process.

We have all heard the saying, "Think globally—act locally," in relation to environmental and political issues. But the approach is a good one to take with writing as well. While working on the individual elements, you are thinking about the larger connections. As you continue writing, individual pieces often begin to flock together and form a book of poems or short stories, or a "novel in stories," as you recognize and build on recurring themes.

* * *

- Often, it is hard to find the center of our own pieces. Workshops with other writers can be useful not only for refining a piece, but for suggesting different ways one might "re-cast" a certain subject as well.

- You might also exchange your journals, perhaps after a free-write. Have your reader identify any structure which might be emerging, voices which haven't been heard, stories which need to be expanded. You might also note the most compelling lines or images, the heart of the piece. Have additional readers do the same.

(See *Genre to Genre.*)

Writing by Heart

In Paule Marshall's essay "Poets in the Kitchen," she speaks of the poetry she inherited from her Barbadan heritage by listening to the talk in the kitchen. She says that these early lessons in narrative trained her ear. Her stories and the rhythms of her writing had their roots in the language of her house. Similarly, Amy Tan says in "Mother Tongue" that she sought to capture from her mother's Chinese and "broken" English what "language ability tests can never reveal: her intent, her passion, her imagery, the rhythms of her speech and the nature of her thoughts."

Listen for the rhythms of your lineage. Listen for the poems and stories in your house. Try to access the ones in your memory. We have all been participants in an oral tradition from which we can draw.

Listen, also, for the memories which might be stirred by unexpected conversations or connections. In a recent workshop, one participant wrote a short piece about talking with her grandmother on the way to a hair appointment. The piece ended with her dropping the grandmother off. A few readers said they felt somewhat disappointed for not being taken into the salon. Someone in the group, scoffing slightly, commented, "What could happen in a salon?"

Another student then responded that many of his most memorable childhood moments took place in his friend's mother's salon, and I suggested he write about that for his next piece. In his first attempt, one could sense a wealth of stories hidden in each sentence. As we talked, he realized that he had layers of material from the experiences at the salon. The years he spent there, from eleven to fifteen were also a significant detail—a particularly formative time in his life. Even the salon's name, *Mystiques*, couldn't have been more appropriate:

> ...There were local politicians, insurance salesmen, car dealers, janitors, ball players, teachers, policemen, drug dealers, dog owners, computer specialists...We made them feel like kings and queens on spinning thrones...Sabrian and I

built a smaller refuge in the back of the shop...Boxes of products with descriptions like dark, lovely, and silky cluttered the floor. Here, we set up shop. There were basketball games of the century played with balls of electrical tape and triple rims made of hangers. We stood upon economy-sized buckets of hair grease to get the height needed for a regulation inside court.

— Courtney Chew, UM

For later pieces, I suggested he write from the different voices of the people who came through the salon. He also had a much longer story to tell about the back room. He realized the salon was the perfect setting for exploring the patchwork of his childhood memories and lineage. One could see the threads of many stories which could be woven together in a much larger work: a book of poetry, short stories, a novel.

* * *

- Access your own oral history. Write about your own "poets in the kitchen," or the toolshed, or the salon, or the corner of Fifth and Main. Try to capture the rhythms of speech from your heritage. (See *History, Herstory.*)

- Learning poems by heart is another way to honor our oral traditions. As a child, are there any poems you learned by heart? Think of what the words suggest: "by heart." We enter a poem more fully when we make it part of our memory. We claim it as our own. In a workshop, have everyone in your group share a favorite poem. In your recitations, try to inhabit the poem as fully as possible with your voice. Later, share one you have written yourself and have committed to memory.

- Write a short piece about a poem (or song) you remember. Why do you remember it? Some students have commented that they only remember advertising jingles. One said that her TV was her "poet in the kitchen." Even this sort of recognition could be the start of something.

Writing for Your Life

Anna Akhmatova spoke of the conditions of her life in Stalin-era Russia as influencing her decision to be a poet rather than, perhaps, a novelist. To sustain a long work, she said, one would need larger spaces of uninterrupted time, a semblance of order, "drawers," a life with fewer interruptions. It is, perhaps, this reality which has at least partially influenced the work of many poets in exile or conditions of political turmoil, as they had to, literally or metaphorically, write their words on the run.

Though privileged to live in a society free from the immediacy of war or political upheaval, many of us spend years overworked, underpaid, balancing several jobs to make ends meet, our energies scattered. We may write poems because they burn to be released, and also because we may be able to draft them in a relatively small space of time.

It depends on the individual, of course. If you have all the time and order in the world, it does not necessarily mean that you will produce tomes. And sometimes, an over-burdened schedule can actually make a person manage time far more efficiently. Chaotic conditions sometimes provide the force or energy behind the art, but they can also greatly hinder a writer.

Many writers have written about the interruptions which kept them from their work. Samuel Taylor Coleridge's famous fragment, "Kubla Khan," remains a fragment because Coleridge was interrupted by some business matter and could never finish the poem (this account may well be a fiction, though; see *Completing Kubla Khan*). In Tess Gallagher's "I Stop Writing the Poem," the speaker does so to "fold the clothes." Virginia Woolf, conscious of such hindrances for women writers in particular, articulated the need for a "room of one's own" to allow the creative spirit to thrive.

* * *

- Make a schedule. Give yourself a set time to write. Commit to a certain amount of words or pages each day, or every other day, depending on the reality of your life. You will be surprised by how much you have to say and how the words add up. Once you have the words on the page, you have something to work with, something to reshape and re-form.

- Try freewriting about the conditions of your life over the years and how you think they may have affected the form and content of your writing. When have you been the most productive? What have been your "interruptions"? Often, they are the "life" which gives your "art" substance.

Ars Poetica

Every writer, at some point, feels the need to articulate something about the act of writing itself. For poets, a poem with this purpose is known as *Ars Poetica* (Art of Poetry). A definition of poetry might begin as a poem about something else, or even a poem which rejects the art. Marianne Moore's famous poem, "Poetry," begins: "I, too, dislike it: there are things that are more important be-yond/all this fiddle." The poem, however, works toward an articulation of what Moore sees as genuine: the "imaginary gardens with real toads in them."

Several poets' articulations have become famous comments on the art:

> "a way of remembering what it would impoverish us to forget."
> —Robert Frost (1874–1963)

> "A poem should not mean, but be."
> —Archibald Macleish (1892–1982)

> "If I feel physically as if the top of my head were taken off, I know that it is poetry."
> —Emily Dickinson (1830–1886)

> "Poetry is music written for the human voice."
> —Maya Angelou (b. 1928)

> "Poetry is prose bewitched."
> —Mina Loy (1882–1966)

> "hundreds of things coming together at the right moment."
> —Elizabeth Bishop (1911–1979)

> "something that penetrates for an instant into the unconscious."
> —Robert Bly (b. 1926)

A major element of poetry is transformation. Writing can have the power to transform one thing into another, something ugly into something beautiful, through language. Robert Pinsky comments that if you think a subject is "unpoetic," that you couldn't possibly write a poem about it, then "that's your challenge."

W.H. Auden once wrote, "Poetry makes nothing happen." But perhaps that statement derives from the way our culture has become so removed from poetry. Redefining poetry can be one step towards reclaiming it.

* * *

- Write your own definitions of poetry. In a workshop, have participants read their definitions one after another, as a single poem. Inevitably, some will be more abstract, some concrete, some serious, some more lighthearted. These juxtapositions create an effect of their own, and the series of voices opens discussion about the communal nature of writing. The following are examples from my workshops with children:

    "Poetry is when you are walking on a sidewalk that is invisible,
    and there is a hole, and you fall because
    you stare at something you see."
        — Claudia, 3rd grade

    "Poetry is a dog running away from a cat."
        —Ricardo Navarro, 3rd grade

    "Poetry is visualizing something and writing it down
    to show others. Kind of like sleeping in air and having
    to fall down to write. Sometimes I'm like flying around
    the world spinning around until my head falls off."
        —Vanessa Valladares, 3rd grade

    "Poetry is like when a baby comes out from her mom."
        —Mayra Ortiz, 3rd grade

    "Poetry is like a bus going to an island."
    Poetry is like an island going to a bus.
        —Hilda Grande, 3rd grade

    "Poetry is crossing a rickety old bridge,
    and a plank breaks beneath you."
        —Eric Klein, 4th grade

"Poetry is a house that's burning down in a thunderstorm.
It's a flower growing out of a brick.
It's an adjustable sun, so you don't get burnt.
It's a dark house, with one light on."
　　—Holly Castillo, 6th grade

"Poetry is like a skull rising from the grave,
a flower blooming at midnight.
Poetry is two words meeting at a different place at the same time."
　　—Tracey Carter, 8th grade

- Take Pinsky's challenge. Choose the most "unpoetic" subject you can think of, and write a poem about it. Richard Wilbur's (b. 1921) "Junk" and "Love Calls Us to the Things of This World" are good examples of this, with their depiction of garbage and laundry, respectively:

An axe angles
　　　　　from my neighbor's ashcan...
The shivered shaft
　　　　　rises from a shellheap
Of plastic playthings,
　　　　　paper plates...

　　　　　　*

Oh, let there be nothing on earth but laundry,
Nothing but rosy hands in the rising steam
And clear dances done in the sight of heaven.

Lucille Clifton's "Homage to My Hips" and Maxine Kumin's "The Excrement Poem" are two other examples of *Ars(e) Poetica*, perhaps:

We eat, we evacuate, survivors that we are.
I think these things each morning with shovel
and rake, drawing the risen brown buns
toward me, fresh from the horse oven, as it were...

...coprinus mushrooms spring up in a downpour.
I think of what drops from us and must then
be moved to make way for the next and next...
　　—Maxine Kumin (b. 1925)

How You Say a Thing

What you say is important, of course, but *how* you say it often makes the difference. As Robert Frost says,

> I don't suppose the water's changed at all.
> You and I know enough to know it's warm
> Compared with cold, and cold compared with warm.
> But all the fun's in how you say a thing.

The "how" is made up of a great variety of elements operating simultaneously: *diction* (word choice), *syntax* (the arrangement of words—from the Greek, meaning arrange together), figurative language, form. Each of these elements contributes to the *tone* (the stance or attitude) of the piece. Titles might be used to set up the tone from the beginning.

Although some exercises in this book suggest ways to use words in fresh, innovative, sometimes surreal arrangements, diction certainly need not be difficult or bizarre to have a powerful effect. (See *The Man-Moth*, *Hoppergrass*, *Dream Logic*.) Consider the following well-known poem by Robert Frost with new eyes and ears. Read it aloud to appreciate its full impact.

ROBERT FROST (1874-1963)

The Road Not Taken

Two roads diverged in a yellow wood,
And sorry I could not travel both
And be one traveler, long I stood
And looked down one as far as I could
To where it bent in the undergrowth;

Then took the other, as just as fair,
And having perhaps the better claim,
Because it was grassy and wanted wear;
Though as for that the passing there
Had worn them really about the same,

And both that morning equally lay
In leaves no step had trodden black.
Oh! I kept the first for another day!
Yet knowing how way leads on to way,
I doubted if I should ever come back.

I shall be telling this with a sigh
Somewhere ages and ages hence:
Two roads diverged in a wood, and I —
I took the one less traveled by,
And that has made all the difference.

The choice of simple, but precise words in the poem, such as *diverged, undergrowth, traveler*, and *way*, build the poem's intensity. One of the most evocative lines in the poem is "Yet knowing how way leads on to way"—an inventive syntax which repeats the most simple of words: *way*. Notice, also, how Frost keeps the rhyme fresh by using different parts of speech (noun, adjective, verb, noun adverb, pronoun, preposition) at the end of each line. (See *Committing a Rhyme*.)

Frost's poem also builds on a single image. It extends one central metaphor. Use of specific images and figurative language are essential qualities of poetry and prose, means by which abstract ideas become concrete. Specificity can actually have a far greater power of universality than vague abstractions. If you write, for instance, about one very specific loss and inhabit the experience with vivid, descriptive language, it will have more far-reaching effects than if you speak about loss in the abstract. (Note Elizabeth Bishop's treatment of loss in "One Art" in *Villanelle*.) One old rule of writing bears repeating: Show, don't just tell. A little "telling" is sometimes essential, as long as it is kept in balance with the "showing," and doesn't merely re-state or replace the image.

All good creative writing is based on sensory experience. We often think of images as being visual, but they are also auditory, tactile, olfactory, and gustatory as well. Many exercises in the book aid in enhancing figurative language by using all of the senses (*Natural Comparisons, Through the Window, Feelers First, Natural Tunes, Art Speaks, Define the Color Blue, Anonymous Album*, etc.).

Good imagery reveals something with new eyes and ears and hands and turns it around for examination, as in H.D.'s words from "The Moon in Your Hands":

> If you take the moon in your hands
> and turn it round
> (heavy slightly tarnished platter)
> you're there...
>
> perceiving the other-side of everything,
> mullein leaf, dogwood-leaf, moth-wing
> and dandelion-seed under the ground.
> —H.D. (1886-1961)

CARL SANDBURG (1878-1967)

Fog

The fog comes
on little cat feet.
It sits looking
over harbor and city
on silent haunches
and then moves on.

EZRA POUND (1885-1972)

In a Station of the Metro

The apparition of these faces in the crowd;
Petals on a wet, black bough.

Although every good writer uses imagery, the above poems are examples of "Imagist" poetry. (The Imagists flourished particularly between 1908-1917 and included such poets as Wallace Stevens, William Carlos Williams, H.D., Carl Sandburg, Ezra Pound, and Marianne Moore.) Pound first wrote his famous two-line poem as a thirty-line piece, but later found the "one-image" poem captured more than a page of words in this case—a single almost cinematic image (slowed down by the "apparition") which would reverberate afterwards. He thought of the poem as "haiku-like."

The following is a brief review of types of figurative language, with examples of poetry and prose. Most of the terms derive from the Greek (which gives them their unwieldy quality in English). The technique, not the terms themselves, are the essential element, although you will probably also learn the terms, as you try your hand at them:

apostrophe: addressing something not usually spoken to: an historical figure, a poem, an object, an idea, something in nature.

> Now, you great stanza, you heroic mould,
> Bend to my will, for I must give you love:
> —Louise Bogan (1897-1970)

> Milton! Thou shouldst be living at this hour.
> —William Wordsworth (1770-1850)

(Further examples from William Blake and William Butler Yeats are in *Dear Star, Do You Know the Moon?*)

personification: giving human characteristics to something non-human (an animal, inanimate object, abstract idea, etc.).

> A tattered coat upon a stick, unless
> Soul clap its hands and sing, and louder sing
> For every tatter in its mortal dress...
> —William Butler Yeats (1865-1939)

> The great crane still swung its black arm from Oxford Street to above their heads.
> —Doris Lessing (b. 1919)

(See *Natural Tunes, Inhabitation*.)

synesthesia: (from Greek, meaning blended feeling) the association of an image perceived by one of the senses with one perceived by another.

> ...if I could touch you
> my hands would begin to sing...
> —Mary Oliver (b. 1935)

...Or will the smell
be dried and baked into ribbons
against a rusty knife?
　　　—Joy Harjo (b. 1951)

(See *Define the Color Blue*.)

hyperbole: exaggeration (from the Greek, throwing beyond).

I'll love you dear, I'll love you
Till China and Africa meet,
And the river jumps over the mountain,
And the salmon sing in the street.
　　　—W.H. Auden (1907-1973)

And from far up, ringing from peak to peak of the summits over
us, came a cry of such unutterable and ecstatic joy that it sounds
down across the years and tingles among the cups of my quiet
breakfast table.
　　　—Loren Eiseley (1907-1977)

understatement: something phrased in a restrained way.

...for destruction ice
Is also great
and would suffice
　　　—Robert Frost (1874-1963)

litotes: (from the Greek, plain or meager) a type of understatement
which makes a point by denying the opposite, such as "He's no
angel."

for life's not a paragraph
and death i think is no parentheses.
　　　—e.e. cummings (1894-1962)

metonymy: referring to something by using the name of
something associated with it. (the Church, the Crown, the White
House, the silver screen). There are many categories of metonymy,
such as using the name of the place for the institution: "Wall Street
is jittery," or the object for the user: "the factories are on strike."
Note how scepter, crown, scythe, and spade represent social
classes in the following passage:

Scepter and crown must tumble down
And in the dust be equal made
With the poor crooked scythe and spade.
—James Shirley (1596-1666)

synecdoche: (from the Greek, taking whole) a type of metonymy, in which a part refers to the whole.

The hand that signed the paper felled a city.
—Dylan Thomas (1914-1953)

Letters

Every day brings a ship,
Every ship brings a word;
Well for those who have no fear,
Looking seaward well assured
That the word the vessel brings
Is the word they wish to hear.
—Ralph Waldo Emerson (1803-1882)

paradox: (from the Greek meaning contrary to expectation) a statement which seems like a contradiction, but which reveals another layer of truth. Shakespeare's poetry is filled with paradox.

When most I wink, then do mine eyes best see...
All days are nights to see till I see thee.

When my love swears she is made of truth
I do believe her, though I know she lies.
—William Shakespeare (1564-1616)

Twenty men crossing a bridge,
Into a village
Are twenty men crossing twenty bridges,
Into twenty villages,
Or one man
Crossing a single bridge into a village.
—Wallace Stevens (1879-1955)

Sylvie did not want to lose me. She did not want me to grow gigantic and multiple, so that I seemed to fill the whole house.

And below is always the accumulated past, which vanishes but does not vanish, which perishes and remains.
—Marilynne Robinson (b. 1944)

oxymoron: compressed paradox, like "jumbo shrimp," or "sweet sorrow."

Parting is such sweet sorrow.
—William Shakespeare (1564-1616)

allusion: reference to another literary work, history, art, event, etc. An allusion might be direct or subtle. Sometimes a work declares an influence directly, such as the quotation from Dante which opens T.S. Eliot's "Love Song of J. Alfred Prufrock." Names are another method of creating allusion, such as Melville's choice of the Biblical tyrant Ahab for the captain in *Moby Dick*.

An allusion might also be more subtle, such as the use of a quotation or a paraphrase from another author within the piece. Sometimes the allusion has an archetypal quality about it, which recalls an age-old story, such as the reference to the Flood in Alice Munro's short story "The Found Boat":

At the end of Bell Street, McKay Street, Mayo Street, there was the Flood. It was the Wawanash River, which every spring overflowed its banks...Light reflected off the water made everything bright and cold, as it is in a lakeside town, and woke or revived in people certain vague hopes of disaster...There were always things floating around in the Flood—branches, fence-rails, logs, road signs, old lumber; sometimes boilers, washtubs, pots and pans, or even a car seat or stuffed chair, as if somewhere the Flood had got into a dump.
—Alice Munro (b. 1931)

(See *Old Myth New Myth*.)

metaphor: a comparison in which something is directly described as being something else.

Young as she is, the stuff
Of her life is great cargo
—Richard Wilbur (b. 1921)

> Where is your tribal memory? Sirs,
> in that grey vault. The sea. The sea
> has locked them up. The sea is History.
>> —Derek Walcott (b. 1930)

> You are the lonely gathering of rivers
> below the plane that left you in Ohio;
> you are the fog of language on Manhattan
> where it's descending.
>> —Marilyn Hacker (b. 1942)

extended metaphor: expands on an original metaphor. Many poems operate on this principle, as do many prose passages, sometimes extensive works. Sylvia Plath's "Colossus," for instance, extends the metaphor of her father as an ancient statue, and of herself as a small creature crawling over it:

> ...Scaling little ladders with gluepots and pails of Lysol
> I crawl like an ant in mourning
> Over the weedy acres of your brow...
> Nights I squat in the cornucopia
> Of your left ear, out of the wind...
> The sun rises under the pillar of your tongue...
>> —Sylvia Plath (1932-1963)

Adrienne Rich uses the extended metaphor of an ocean dive to depict a journey into history and into her psyche in "Diving into the Wreck":

> I go down
> rung after rung...
> I came to see the damage that was done
> and the treasures that prevail...
> the thing I came for:
> the wreck and not the story of the wreck
> the thing itself and not the myth.
>> —Adrienne Rich (b. 1929)

(See *Natural Comparisons*.)

simile: a type of metaphor using such words as like, as, seems, appears.

What did we say to each other
that now we are as the deer
who walk in single file
    —N. Scott Momaday (b. 1934)

What happens to a dream deferred?
Does it dry up
like a raisin in the sun?
    —Langston Hughes (1902-1967)

implied metaphor: uses neither a connective such as "like" nor a form of the verb "to be."

...telephones crouch, getting ready to ring
In locked up offices.
    —Philip Larkin (1922-1985)

In Mississippi I wandered among some of the ghosts and bones, and it is my great lesson to have learned to stop trying to evade and forget what I have seen and heard and understood and now must know, but rather to embrace the ghosts and cradle the bones and call them my own.
    —Anthony Walton (b. 1960)

analogy: a kind of reasoning (used in the sciences, math, history, and other disciplines as well) which is based on metaphor and crucial to our process of thinking and making connections.

                         But enough
For when we have blamed the wind we can blame love.
    —William Butler Yeats (1865-1939)

Terry Tempest Williams uses analogy and extended metaphor, as well as other figurative language in "Peregrine Falcon" from *Refuge*:

Our urban wastelands are becoming wildlife's last stand. The great frontier. We've moved them out of town like all other low-income tenants...I like to sit on the piles of unbroken Hefties, black bubbles of sanitation...The starlings gorge themselves, bumping into each other like drunks. They are not discretionary.

They'll eat anything, just like us...Perhaps we project on to starlings that which we deplore in ourselves: our numbers, our aggression, our greed, and our cruelty. Like starlings, we are taking over the world.
—Terry Tempest Williams (b. 1955)

Writers often use many figures of speech within a single passage. How many can you identify in the following familiar passage?

from *Macbeth* (Act V, Scene v)

Tomorrow, and tomorrow, and tomorrow
Creeps in this petty pace from day to day
To the last syllable of recorded time;
And all our yesterdays have lighted fools
The way to dusty death. Out, out, brief candle!
Life 's but a walking shadow, a poor player,
That struts and frets his hour upon the stage,
And then is heard no more. It is a tale
Told by an idiot, full of sound and fury,
Signifying nothing.
—William Shakespeare (1564-1616)

Aristotle (384-322 BCE) believed that metaphor (the word is sometimes used to mean all figurative language) was the most important skill. He wrote:

By far the greatest thing is to be a master of metaphor. It is the one thing that cannot be learned from others. It is a sign of genius, for a good metaphor implies an intuitive perception of similarity among dissimilars.

Although Aristotle was likely right in suggesting that mastery of metaphor cannot be learned from others, we all use metaphor in our daily language. Practicing the different means of making figurative language is a way to understand its use, bring it into our own writing, and exercise our ability to draw connections in the world.

* * *

- A fun way to practice these techniques (and simultaneously generate ideas) is to write these terms on scraps of paper and then pick three out of a hat. Write a short piece containing all three elements.

- Take a piece of your own freewriting. Make a list of abstract words contained within, and then practice writing passages using figurative language to convey the concept without ever stating the word. This is a good exercise to use in a workshop as well and might be adapted as follows:

- Each person should write down an abstract emotion or concept: love, anger, nationalism etc. on a scrap of paper. Then scramble the words. Each participant should write for about ten minutes, attempting to depict the concept— through image, dialogue or action—but without ever stating the concept. (It is fun to read these aloud and have people guess the abstract words which initiated them.)

- For a fun, but rather challenging exercise, write down several (or all) of the above types of figurative language on scraps of paper, then select them randomly, and write a poem in which each line contains the device. "Following orders" in this fashion can help you get a grasp on the particular figure of speech, but the random sequence will also provide you with some unique variations which might not have otherwise arisen—lines or thoughts to use later. In some rare instances, the initial results might actually produce a lasting poem. This exercise often yields rather surreal connections. (See *Dream Logic.*)

  For instance, use the devices in the order they are introduced:

42

line:

one (apostrophe):	Address something nonhuman
two (personification):	Personify something.
three (synesthesia):	Use an image mixing sensory perception
four (hyperbole):	Exaggerate
five (understatement/litotes):	Use understatement/deny the opposite
six (metonymy/synecdoche):	Refer to something by using something related/ use a part for a whole
seven (paradox/oxymoron):	Write a contradiction/compressed contradiction
eight (allusion):	Allude to something
nine (metaphor):	Use a metaphor
ten (simile):	Extend the metaphor, using simile
eleven (implied metaphor/analogy):	Extend the metaphor further, using implied metaphor or analogy

For a later, much greater challenge using the above exercise, you might also incorporate rhyme and meter. (See *The Weave of Meter* and *Committing a Rhyme.*)

The following student response uses nearly all of the above devices in the following order: apostrophe, personification, hyperbole, paradox, synecdoche, allusion, simile, metaphor, extended metaphor.

Valentine

O, my blood, you are so red and busy,
You must get frustrated and want a drink.
So I will fix you hundreds of them, for
Alcohol poisoning might make you thin.
Vintage bottles burst forth tiny red cells
Gentle white ones with the power to kill.
Then, a funeral in my platelets,
Empty as E. Dickinson's windowsill.
You, like the silent chair in which she sat.
I more mischievous, a Cheshire cat,
Her cold fingers stroke my mane...life's chess game.
          —Jennifer Pearson, UM

Using too much figurative language in a piece of writing,
of course, might also weigh it down or cause confusion.
Some combinations of metaphor might be useful to create
a surreal effect, but be wary of creating unintentional
mixed or warring metaphors such as "Language is the
river that opens doors" or "the curves on the road
unfolded."

• In a workshop, the above "following orders" exercise might also
   be done as a collaborative poem with a random quality
   (the results will likely be even more surreal than the
   previous exercises). Each person writes the first line, then
   passes the paper to the right. Then each person writes the
   second line, and passes, etc.

(For similar exercises which will yield random, often surreal results,
see *The Man-Moth, Dream Logic, Completing Kubla Khan*.)

A Forest of Symbols

Invariably, when we talk about symbols in workshops, someone will ask such questions as "Isn't a boat ever just a boat?" The question recalls Sigmund Freud's famous answer that "sometimes a cigar is just a cigar." It depends on the context, of course. A car that passes by might just be a car, for instance, but your first car might carry great meaning and symbolism. A symbol (related to the Greek *symbolon*, meaning put together) asks the reader to ascribe a concept or idea (like freedom) to something tangible (like a car).

Symbols vary from culture to culture, depending on religion, history, landscape, and other elements. However, because they also arise out of our unconscious, there are many parallels as well. These "universal" symbols or models, such as a flood, a forest, or a fire are known as archetypes, and often carry a duality of meaning. A flood is both restorative and destructive, a forest is a place of natural beauty but also danger, and fire gives warmth, but has great power to destroy. (See *Dream Logic* and *Old Myth, New Myth.*) Symbols often arrive on their own for a writer, and only later may he or she realize what has happened on the page. They may carry many layers of meaning.

A piece of writing might be overt about its symbolism, or the symbolism might exist more subtly in a piece. An *allegory* is the simplest form of symbolism—a piece in which it is obvious that the elements stand for something. In longer allegorical works, such as Dante's *Divine Comedy*, there are often many layers of meaning and interpretation. Because allegory lends itself especially to didactic writing (work which attempts to teach ethical, moral, or religious values), in the wrong hands, allegory can feel like a sledgehammer to the reader. Overt symbols can easily become loud cymbals if the rest of the music is not kept in balance.

We live in an elaborate symbolic matrix. No one can deny it. We can see the evidence on the average drive to work. Deliberately invented symbols in our society such as words, flags, and road signs are usually referred to by scholars as *signs*. We also have *traditional* or *conventional* symbols, such as flowers or religious icons which have a certain meaning in society and which might appear in a writer's work. Writers might also develop *private* or contextual symbols which develop throughout a single piece (such as the whale in *Moby Dick*) or recur in different works (such as Yeats' many gyres).

Even people might take on a legendary or symbolic quality in a culture (Attila the Hun, Socrates, Mother Theresa, Elvis, John F. Kennedy). Actions are also sometimes symbolic—in real life and on the page. Actions tell a great deal about a person's character. (See *In Character.*)

Although every writer uses some element of symbolism, the label "Symbolist" has been given to a group of nineteenth century French poets, including Rimbaud, Mallarmé, and Baudelaire, the latter speaking of the world as a "forest of symbols."

> from "The Cat"
>
> There is a bow that can so sweep
> That perfect instrument, my heart:
> Or make more sumptuous music start
> From its most vibrant cord and deep,
>
> That can the voice of this strange elf,
> This cat, bewitching and seraphic,
> Subtly harmonious in his traffic
> With all things else, and with himself.
> —Charles Baudelaire (1821-1867)
> (trans. Roy Campbell)

Richard Wilbur's "The Writer" uses a starling's difficult escape from a room as a symbol for the experience of a writer. Although he never explicitly declares the symbolism, the connection is very clear, as the speaker watches the bird, trapped in the room,

> Batter against the brilliance, drop like a glove
> To the hard floor, or the desk-top.
>
> And wait then, humped and bloody,
> For the wits to try it again; and how our spirits
> Rose when, suddenly sure,
>
> It lifted off from a chair-back,
> Beating a smooth course for the right window
> And clearing the sill of the world.

* * *

- Think of an incident which felt symbolic of something else (such as a starling trapped in a room). Write about the incident without declaring what you felt it symbolized. (In a workshop, you might exchange these, and see if your reader can discern the symbolism.)

- In a workshop, look among your possessions for symbolic items. Take out your wallet or purse. What symbolic items do you have in your possession at the moment? Money is a sign for something, of course, but it also functions on a symbolic level. Pictures? A driver's license? Unmentionables? Do you have a piece of jewelry, clothing, a tattoo that is symbolic? Write a short piece which makes the symbolism of the item clear, but subtle. (You might also use symbolic items in your vicinity—a tree, a blackboard, a painting.)

Writing from Nature

This section offers insights and exercises to respond to nature (both "wilderness" and the nature around our own homes) and to cultivate a sense of place.

Through the Window

When I taught writing in the National Science Foundation program, "Ecology for Urban Students," on the first day of class, I asked the students to write about the nature around their homes. Most of them lived in the inner city, so I expected answers like pigeons and cats, spiders in windows. But I was unprepared for one student's response. Her brother had recently been shot, and she wrote about the gang warfare in her neighborhood as the "nature around her home." With her Darwinian answer, she innocently reminded me what different realities these children were living, from me, as well as from each other. I thought I was sensitive to their daily lives, but I realized how much I had to learn. Her perspective on nature cracked something open for me.

Thoreau once said, "It's not a matter of what you look at. It's a matter of what you see." We miss so much in our daily lives. We have all heard the saying, "I'll believe it when I see it." But the reverse is also true: "I'll see it when I believe it." In my workshops, we talk a great deal about perceptual filters, the filters which define what and how we view the world. They are formed by such elements as religion, education, sex, race, and age.

A friend of mine once gave her four-year-old daughter a camera and let her take the pictures at a party. It was fascinating to see the perspective the pictures revealed, the predominance of knees and floor and expressions people made especially for a child.

Tom Wolfe, in his essay "O Rotten Gotham," speaks about the danger of looking at the city from a bird's eye view. The perspective from above distances the urban planner, who does not experience the reality of inner-city congestion, pollution, and noise. His distanced perspective keeps him out of the *behavioral sink*, a term in ethology for the unhealthy outcome of collecting animals together in unusually great numbers.

We have all had the experience of passing something every day and never *seeing* it, that tree at the end of your block, the historical marker around the corner. The phenomenon is not limited to our eyes. When we learn a new word, suddenly we hear it everywhere. And we all know the power a smell has to awaken memories. But metaphors for sight particularly fill our language, our views and visions: "I see what you mean," for instance. In Greek, a term of endearment is *matia mu*, which means "my eyes." You call your love your eyes.

Annie Dillard says, "The lover can see, and the knowledgeable." I remember one hike in particular I took in the Fakahatchee Strand with a group of biologists: an ornithologist, a botanist, a herpetologist. They all focused on different details. The ornithologist was particularly memorable, translating all the bird calls we heard into warnings and desires.

We see so much when we slow our paces, which is probably why we see so much on trips. Everything feels new, worth seeing. But our very homes can be radically different landscapes, if we approach them differently.

Start by looking through your own window. Take a walk in your backyard. Notice the tiny things. Maybe get down on the ground and look from that perspective. Does the world look any different? When we change our perspective, we might see the whole world reflected in the tiniest space and time:

> To see a world in a grain of sand,
> and a heaven in a wildflower.
> To hold infinity in the palm of your hand,
> and eternity in an hour.
> —William Blake (1757-1827)

* * *

- Make a list of the "perceptual filters" which influence your vision (peer group, geography, religion, etc.) Develop a short piece about one or more of the elements on your list.

- Watch for and describe the nature you see around your own home—the dramatic and also the tiny. You might even use a magnifying glass and write from that new perspective. Look at the veins of a leaf, for instance. Where do the tiny roads lead? Describe the details of the world you see. (See *Feelers First.*)

Natural Tunes

WILLIAM BUTLER YEATS (1865-1939)

The Lake Isle of Innisfree

I will arise and go now, and go to Innisfree,
And a small cabin build there, of clay and wattles made:
Nine bean-rows will I have there, a hive for the honey-bee,
And live alone in the bee-loud glade.

And I shall have some peace there, for peace comes dropping slow,
Dropping from the veils of the morning to where the cricket sings;
There midnight's all a glimmer, and noon a purple glow,
And evening full of the linnet's wings.

I will arise and go now, for always night and day
I hear lake water lapping with low sounds by the shore;
While I stand on the roadway, or on the pavements gray,
I hear it in the deep heart's core.

The natural world is filled with songs. We can learn a great deal about the rhythms of nature by just listening. Go to the ocean, a waterfall, a river near your home. Listen for awhile. Then try writing as you listen. How does it affect your rhythm?

Go into the woods and listen to the trees. Listen to the wind in the trees. When I was growing up, my family had a stethoscope at home, which, as a budding botanist, I found could be used to listen to the xylem and phloem, the tides inside the trees.

Stay very still and listen to bird calls for a while. Then write. What might they be saying? Can you tell the tone of their songs? Do you hear the scolding shriek of a bluejay, the wild laugh of a loon, or the lyrical song of a warbler? Do they sound like anything you know?

Some years ago, I awakened to what I perceived to be cats yowling. A few days later, I discovered it was the peacocks near my house. Forever now, when I hear the cries of peacocks, I think of that original association.

I have often driven out to the Everglades at night to look at stars. In the darkness, sounds became all the more poignant. One can hear the grunts of gators and pig frogs filling the night, not to mention the constant buzz of the persistent mosquitos.

You might also be able to discern certain rhythms with your eyes. A good example is a lizard's dewlap. Lizards love the windows of my house. They hold elaborate mating rituals on the outside sills. I have sat, mesmerized by the hypnotic beat of the dewlap concealed in the throat, revealing itself again and again.

Think about your own voice. What physical realities make the sounds and words emerge? Why do people have accents when they speak other languages? Do we train our mouths to move in a certain way? In a favorite novel of mine, David Malouf's *An Imaginary Life*, there is a passage where the Roman poet, Ovid, is teaching a wild boy to speak. The boy can imitate all the birds and animals of the woods, but rather than merely mimicking, he seems to become the creature:

> His whole face is contorted differently as he assumes each creature's voice. If he were to speak always as frog or hawk or wolf, the muscles of his throat and jaw might grow to fit the sound, so intimately are the creatures and the sounds they make connected, so deeply are they one...I have begun to understand him. In imitating the birds, he is not, like our mimics, copying something that is outside him and revealing the accuracy of his ear or the virtuosity of his speech organs. He is being the bird. He is allowing it to speak out of him.
> — David Malouf (b. 1934)

Try making the sounds you hear. What new muscles do you use? One interesting and easy exercise to do in the wild will attract many birds to you. Conceal yourself well and make repeated *psh psh psh* sounds. The sounds imitate the scolding calls of many birds. It can also be a meditative experience to remain still and call like that. Listen to the responses you get. Are there rhythms, repetitions? Imagine yourself as an arriving bird. What are you hearing? What are you thinking as you respond?

In Malouf's book, as Ovid learns more about the wild boy, he realizes how deeply the boy is connected to the universe. If he is to understand the child, he needs to "think as he must: I am raining. I am thundering."

* * *

- Choose any element of your environment and try writing with its voice, such as Ted Hughes does in "Hawk Roosting":

    > I sit in the top of the wood, my eyes closed...
    > My feet are locked upon the rough bark.
    > It took the whole of Creation
    > To produce my foot, my each feather...
    > —Ted Hughes (1930-1998)

- The above exercise makes a good group project as well, one which will emphasize the web of connections. Each person might choose to be a different voice of a certain ecosystem. I have done this exercise with groups of college students as well as young kids. A group of middle school students made a little skit out of the voices, called "The Everglades Council," with the council being made up of various members of the ecosystem. I was pleased to see that students chose to be the tiny things as well as the large: the apple snail and the snail kite, as well as the alligator. Some students chose to be the voice of the sun, the water, the wind. One chose to be the human.

- Another variation on this exercise might be to write through the voice, but make it a riddle of sorts, never directly stating what you are. This is a useful exercise to see if your description is effective.

    (See also *Inhabitation*.)

- In "Ode to a Nightingale," John Keats reflects on the unchanging music of the nightingale throughout history:

    > Perhaps the selfsame song that found a path
    > Through the sad heart of Ruth, when sick for home,
    > She stood in tears amid the alien corn
    > The same that oft-times hath
    > Charmed magic casements, opening on the foam
    > Of perilous seas, in faery lands forlorn.
    > —John Keats (1795-1821)

Let the music in nature take you to another realm. Write about another era in which this song was heard.

• Some words seem to have sounds as their origin—crunch, growl, splash, hum—known as *onomatopoeia*, from the Greek, meaning name-making. A sophisticated use of onomatopoeia can be heard in the following well-known lines by Lord Alfred Tennyson:

> The moan of doves in immemorial elms,
> And murmuring of innumerable bees.

As you listen to sounds around you, repeat the sounds, listening to your own voice for the words which they bring to mind. Keep a list of such words. Incorporate them in a piece of writing.

• Imitate the rhythm of a sound you hear—a bird call, the ocean. Let your form reflect something in the natural world. Robinson Jeffers' long lines, for instance, reflect the rhythm of the dramatic Pacific tides, although, in "Continent's End," he acknowledges an even more ancient rhythm:

> The tides are in our veins, we still mirror the stars, life is your
>   child...
> Mother though my song's measure is like your surf-beat's
>   ancient rhythm I never learned it of you.
> Before there was any water there were tides of fire, both our
>   tones flow from the older fountain.
> —Robinson Jeffers (1887-1962)

• You might also listen for the rhythms of something other than the natural world. Let the rhythms of everyday speech find their way into your writing. (See *Eavesdropping* and *Writing by Heart*.) You might also try to capture the pace of the city—the positives or the negatives. (See Tom Wolfe's use of the chaotic run-on sentence to depict this pace in *The Grammar of the Situation*.)

Feelers First

Rachel Carson said, "It's not as important to know as to feel." We often tend to rely on certain senses more than others. A good exercise in a natural setting is to arrange a "blind" experience. Have your partner blindfold you and lead you through a place. Have fifteen-minute periods of "blindness," during which you touch the bark of trees, the smooth or soft or rough leaves. Do you notice any peculiar smells? Try focusing on one sense at a time. The woods at night carry a certain mystery, partially because our other less-noticed senses become awakened.

In a workshop, you might bring objects into class—either from the natural world, or man-made, if you like. Have participants close their eyes, or blindfold themselves, and touch the objects. Afterwards, describe them on paper. You might choose objects less likely to be recognized or ones that will be recognized easily. Describe them in your journal using only tactile images.

In one recent exercise, I had the students close their eyes and touch the objects I handed them. On the first round, I gave them all the same object: pumice stones, which I thought would make for an interesting experiment. After the students felt them for a few minutes, I then retrieved the stones and asked participants to describe the object and give it a name, based on its physical properties. For the same object, a great variety of names appeared:

> Dusty Trunk, Powdery, Left from a Dinosaur, Sandstone Meteor, Lava Rock, Sculptor's Joy, Porous, Piece of the Moon, Earthy Mineral, Rocky Light, Too Light, Rough and Tough, Sandy, Sponge-Dried, Residue Air.

I then gave everyone another object. I asked the students to use all of their senses except for sight to describe them. The following are a few of the initial descriptions, some of which evolved into longer pieces:

coconut palm husk: Brittle fabric with a loose weave. It had a musty smell like twine. Maybe a piece of burlap sack (Hilary Packin, UM). A piece of fragile cloth (Fred Sherman, UM). Flat and straw-like—a crudely woven piece of material...the edges were frayed like a rough straw mat (Beth Chiofalo, FIU).

a nautilus shell: Hollow and thin, a spiral. It smelled of the tide coming in. Inside was soft, like an ear (Jose Torres, FIU).

curled seed pod: I thought of the double helix of a DNA strand as it spiralled through my fingers (Cris Farinas, FIU).

heliconia flower: I hope it was not the claw of some animal...a complex architecture...it felt lifeless, yet did not smell lifeless. It smelled like a tropical fruit (Alessandra Gherardi, FIU).

cypress knee: A small wooden replica of a mountain. I could feel the crevice of a cave and tip of the highest point. It seemed to have been recently carved. It felt like it took a lot of time to make (Courtney Chew, UM).

acorn: At first I thought it was a tooth, part smooth, part bumpy, pointy at the tip (Michelle Bynum, UM).

*　*　*

• Describe an object (fruit, flower, or object such as the above) using any of your senses except sight. In a "blind workshop," interesting associations might sometimes arise (possibly, even, from mistaking the object), such as the heliconia "claw" above, the acorn as "tooth" or the material "woven" by nature. Perhaps the earliest human weavers took their example from nature.

• Afterwards, you may describe the object using visual imagery. You will have a richer description for the use of all of your senses.

blue porter weed leaf: Shaped like an arrowhead, fine lines when held up to the light. Almost microscopic holes reveal its succulent taste. Some little insect has chosen to feast (Jen Pearson, UM).

staghorn fern: It has veins like a human. On the reverse side there is brown fur, which probably has a more important function than ours. It seems to be reaching out for something (Courtney Chew, UM).

• Write a brief biography (or autobiography) of your object. Go back into its biological ancestry if you like:

> *oak leaf:* I came from a community service session in a Miami High School. Kids took my Dad and covered him with dirt. From one of his twigs, I was born this year—along with my 19,572 brothers...(Jaime Rodriguez, UM).

> *sponge:* I lived a short life in the depths of a cold dark sea. Other creatures were constantly trying to hide in my cavernous body, which brought many predators my way... (Hilary Packin, UM).

• Pretend your object is sacred in our culture. Describe why it is sacred.

> *coconut palm husk:* Each individual part of the weave represents each individual. It shows that everyone's action affects everyone else. The strength of the individual affects the strength of the whole bond... (Courtney Chew, UM).

(See also *Bottle, Baseball, Bra.*)

Revisit Your Hometown

I never wanted to claim Miami Beach as my hometown. It seemed like a neon city to me, a man-made place. Even the land had been dredged out of the ocean. But later, I came to realize that growing up in Miami Beach was part of my heritage, and worth writing about. My change of perspective began with a line I wrote one day: "My hometown was dredged from the bottom of the ocean."

One thing which led me back to South Florida was the extent and proximity of the untamed wilderness: the Everglades, the ocean. Sometimes we need to go away from our homes in order to see them with new eyes.

Many of my college students, though born in Miami, had never been to the Everglades, even though the wilderness is not more than an hour and a half driving from anywhere in the city. South Florida has a kind of rootless quality—many people move quickly through. And the ones who stay usually confine themselves to the city. So it didn't surprise me at all that the middle school inner-city kids had not been there, either. The "Ecology for Urban Students" program gave many of them their first experience outside of their concrete landscape.

We took trips out to the Everglades and Fairchild Tropical Garden, but we started with the nature right outside our doors. Just outside the building where the class met was a natural sinkhole, a dip in the limestone common in Florida. I often held class in the "solution hole," as we called it, where we would be visited by birds and squirrels and occasionally, admittedly less-welcome creatures.

Approaching your hometown from different angles will let you see it both as a specific entity and a place which represents the connections and tensions between nature and culture around the world. What questions might you want to ask about your hometown? Are there any political incidents which you think define it? How are they connected with the geography, the climate?

Your memories and questions are likely to lead you towards further research, into archives. Start with what you do know about your hometown. You will be surprised how many of your pre-conceptions get shaken up. Look for original sources. It can be very exciting to hold first editions and letters in your hand. There is an immediacy about a letter which can be very inspiring. (See *Letters Sent or Unsent.*) In workshops, I have often shared Ernest Hemingway's account of the 1935 hurricane in Key West, which took so many lives. He wrote it first as a letter and then as an article:

> We were the first into Camp Five of the veterans who were working on the highway construction. Out of 187 only 8 survived. Saw more dead than I'd seen in one place since the lower Piave in June of 1918.
>
> The veterans in those camps were practically murdered. The Florida East Coast had a train ready for nearly twenty four hours to take them off the Keys. The people in charge are said to have wired Washington for orders. Washington wired Miami Weather Bureau which is said to have replied there was no danger and it would be a useless expense. The train did not start until the storm started. It never got within thirty miles of the two lower camps. The people in charge of the veterans and the weather bureau can split the responsibility between them.
>
> What I know and can swear to is this: that while the storm was at its height on Matecumbe and most of the people already dead the Miami bureau sent a warning of winds of gale strength on the keys from Key Largo to Key West and of hurricane intensity in the Florida straights [straits] below Key West. They lost the storm completely...

Hemingway's eyewitness testimony has a distinctive energy of its own.

The following are a few children's responses to exercises about South Florida's most frequent natural disaster:

Hurricane

I saw you hurricane,
I saw your rage and fury,
You continued on and on,
For what seemed like eternity,
Then peace.
Everything stopped,
Not a sound was heard
For what seemed like seconds,
Then the rage and fury started again,
And I thought to myself,
Why those torturing seconds of peace?
As the rage and fury increased,
So did my fear....
　　　　—Salomon Tenenbaum, age 12

The Wind

Wind! Wind! Blowing strong
All day, all night, very long
In the distance, I hear the wind
Over the river, around the bend.
Why do you make hurricanes?
Why do you make tornadoes?
You blow over trees.
knock people to their knees.
　　　　—Anonymous, 3rd grade, Mrs. Gonzalez

*　　*　　*

• Return to your hometown, even if you have never left. Try to see it as you have never seen it before. Visit the natural regions of your hometown. Describe what you see. Look up the geological, natural, and human history. Focus on the names of places. Research their origin. Do you find any ironies in them? (See *Nomenclature.*) Have there been any natural phenomena which have defined the place: floods, hurricanes, droughts? Have you experienced them? What images do you remember?

- Think about how landscape helps to shape identity. Do you have more than one place you consider home? Write about how the places you have lived have influenced who you are. Focus on elements such as climate, culture, history, etc.

Natural Comparisons

Writers listen for language and ideas, and the connections often arrive on their own. I love the moment in *Il Postino*, the Academy-award winning film about Chilean poet Pablo Neruda living in exile on an Italian island. He asks the young man who brings his mail for an adjective to describe the island's nets. "Sad," the man responds. It wasn't what Neruda expected, perhaps, but exactly what he was seeking for "Leaning into the Afternoons": "I cast my sad nets toward your oceanic eyes..."

I enjoy taking people to natural places for the first time, because they make me see nature with new eyes. Children, in particular, can make the experience even more magical. On one trip to the Big Cypress Preserve, one little girl commented that the cypress roots looked like knees. The roots are, in fact, called cypress knees, which made me think a great deal about the way things are named. (See *Nomenclature.*) Metaphor, of course, has everything to do with the common names of things. Another child said all the cypress knees together looked like a village of dwarves and proceeded to notice the different features of each of them. Together, they began to name them, making further associations: Grumpy, Sleepy, Mr. Hammons, someone's father, Doctor Simmons.

The word *metaphor* comes from the Greek, meaning to carry over. In Greece, I noticed that moving trucks bear the word *Metafores* on the side. The mind organizes material by trying to link something new to what it already knows. It wants to make metaphor. We speak in metaphor many times a day, without even realizing it. Sometimes, as I begin to talk about the term in a class and ask the class to give me one, they sit searching their minds, before someone finally comes up with a meager one. And yet, they have all probably used several rich ones in their last conversation. Metaphor fills our language, from our daily accounts to our insults to our terms of endearment.

* * *

- Write about an animal you resemble. I have often thought that people resemble certain animals, either by sheer physical appearance or by their actions. We all have our bear-like friends, our nervous, hopping sparrows, our darting lizards, languid cats.

- Compare humans in general to some other animal or plant. One student's rather insightful response compared humans to the maleluca, a water sucking exotic plant originally introduced to help dry up the Everglades, but now threatening the entire ecosystem, as it spreads swiftly through the region and wipes away native plants. The comparison led into a good discussion about the dangers of introducing exotics into an ecosystem and helped others see the effect humans are having on the world.

- Compare the act of writing to something in nature, using an extended metaphor. This kind of exercise also helps one realize how techniques of poetry can be used for more expository purposes. The following excerpts were written by groups of twelve-year-olds in the "Ecology for Urban Students" program:

    Writing is like a beehive because every bee goes out and looks for an idea. All the bees have specific jobs, like words.

    Writing is an ecosystem. It is filled with information about life. The animals and plants in the ecosystem make up the story of the planet. The "eco" is like a story because everything has to work together or it won't work at all. There are different parts just as in a book, but all are connected.

    Writing is like the wind. It takes you places you have never been before, scattering seeds...

    Writing is like fire. They both start out with a spark, then get hotter and hotter, larger and larger. They both spread over great distances. Fire is what makes some plants be able to scatter seeds.

Writing is like a river because events could happen fast and take a sudden turn. One minute everything could appear steady, and the next, the river becomes rapids. It is constantly changing. You can start out at one point and finish in a totally different setting. They are both unpredictable. And when the river reaches the ocean, it is the end of the story—or maybe the beginning.

(See *How You Say a Thing.*)

Nomenclature

I love the common names of plants: Trumpetvine, Goldenrod, Spider Lily. I admit, I never much enjoyed the scientific terms, when I learned them dutifully in my classes. I have always been intrigued by the way things were named, how the act itself was poetry, creating metaphor. A dictionary (the *Oxford English Dictionary* in particular) is a great source for poetry, for tracing the origins of words. A single word can feel like a poem when you find it. In searching for the origin of the word "whale" some years ago, I came across an Old English metaphor for the ocean—*hwael-weg* (whale-road)—which I later used as a central image in a poem. The word is a kind of metaphor known as a kenning, a way of knowing something.

Nomenclature, then, is itself a way of "kenning" the world. Our environments are filled with such poems. Sometimes, I like being in a new environment, where I don't know even the common names of things. Sometimes, the very association I myself make ends up being the common name. When I spent some time in the Pacific Coast rainforest of Colombia some years ago, Salazar, a local who knew all the flora, guided us through the forest. I liked his method of presenting the plants, often asking me what I thought it looked like. I remember one flower which looked like a little hat. It was aptly called *sombrerito del Diablo* (little hat of the Devil). He also showed us the rubber tree with a white milk-like substance inside, which was called the *lechero*, in reference to the milk.

The ironies in names can also be many. Our country is filled with Native American names: Mississippi, Massachusetts, Miami. The names of developments often bear the name of what has been removed in their construction: Mahogany Hammock, Sawgrass Mills Mall.

Other names are puzzling, or suggest stories. On one trip, I drove through a bleak and isolated town in North Dakota named "Climax." On that same trip, I hiked past "Froze" to "Death Creek "and "Hissing Fork Pass" in Montana.

People are often more attuned to the world and more likely to make such observations when traveling. But notice the names in your own towns as well.

*   *   *

- Collect names that you find intriguing: of plants, streets, towns, housing developments. Research their origins. See what develops: a poem, a story, an essay about the names of things.

- Create a myth about how something received its name. Rudyard Kipling's *Just So Stories* are a good example of this.

- Think about your own "nomenclature." Is there a story of your first name? There is certainly a story of your surname, one which might awaken some serious thought about your ancestry.

Hoppergrass

One twelve-year-old girl gave me the idea for the following exercise. She had written about the hoppergrass, the name she had given the grasshopper. That day, I had all the students flip words around. We made a list of some of the words, which we read aloud:

Hoppergrass

lifewild
flybutter
grownover
fedunder
lesschild
lesscare
grass-saw
dozerbull
centershopping
stormthunder
fallrain
flyfire
lightmoon
gladesever

Turning each word around gave it a new kind of resonance. E.E. Cummings loved word play and the sounds of words. "Anyone Lived in a Pretty How Town" is one of my favorites. It is a nature poem, a love poem, a poem about the existential experience, a poem carried by sound.

When I first came across the lines in the poem, "He sang his didn't. He danced his did," somehow, I knew instinctively this was a philosophy of life I wanted to follow:

anyone lived in a pretty how town
(with up so floating many bells down)
spring summer autumn winter
he sang his didn't he danced his did.

Women and men (both little and small)
cared for anyone not at all
they sowed their isn't they reaped their same
sun moon stars rain...
—e.e. cummings (1894-1962)

Try opening the language, in poetry, like e.e. Cummings, or in prose, like James Joyce. At this point, you might not want to sustain it for as long as, say, Joyce's 628 pages of *Finnegan's Wake*, though, which begins:

> riverrun, past Eve and Adam's, from swerve of shore to bend of bay, brings us by a commodius vicus of recirculation back to Howth Castle and Environs. Sir Tristram, violer d'amores, fr'over the short sea, had passencore rearrived from NorthArmorica on this side the scraggy isthmus of Europe Minor to wielderfight his penisolate war: nor had topsawyer's rocks by the stream Oconee exaggerated themselse to Laurens County's gorgios while they went doublin their mumper all the time: nor avoice from afire bellowed mishe mishe to tauftauf thuartpeatrick: not yet, though venissoon after, had a kidscad buttended a bland old isaac: not yet, though all's fair in vanessy, were sosie sesthers wroth with twone nathandjoe. Rot a peck of pa's malt had Jhem or Shen brewed by arclight and rory end to the regginbrow was to be seen ringsome on the aquaface.

> Thefall(bababadalgharaghtakamminarronnkonnbronntonnerronntuonnthunntrovarrhounawnskawntoohoohoordenenthurnuk!) of a once wall-straight oldparr is retaled early in bed and later on life down through all christian minstrelsy.The great fall of the offwall entailed at such short notice the pftjschute of Finnegan, erse solid man, that the humptyhillhead of humself prumptly sends an unquiring one well to the west in quest of his tumptytumtoes:and their upturnpikepointandplace is at the knock out in the park where oranges have been laid to rust upon the green since devlinsfirst loved livvy.

After *Finnegan's Wake*, Lewis Carroll's classic, "The Jabberwocky" seems like plain English. Despite its many made-up words, the events of the story are clear, possibly because of the archetypal pattern of the slaying of a dragon, the conflict of David and Goliath. (See *Old Myth, New Myth*)

LEWIS CARROLL (1832-1898)

Jabberwocky

'Twas brillig, and the slithy toves
 Did gyre and gimble in the wabe;
All mimsy were the borogoves,
 And the mome raths outgrabe.

"Beware the Jabberwock, my son!
 The jaws that bite, the claws that catch!
Beware the Jubjub bird, and shun
 The frumious Bandersnatch!"

He took his vorpal sword in hand:
 Long time the manxome foe he sought —
So rested he by the Tumtum tree,
 And stood awhile in thought.

And as in uffish thought he stood,
 The Jabberwock, with eyes of flame,
Came whiffling through the tulgey wood,
 And burbled as it came!

One, two! One, two! And through and through
 The vorpla blade went snicker-snack!
He left it dead, and with its head
 He went galumphing back.

"And hast thou slain the Jabberwock?
 Come to my arms, my beamish boy!
O frabjous day! Callooh! Callay!"
 He chortled in his joy.

'Twas brillig, and the slithy toves
 Did gyre and gimble in the wabe;
All mimsy were the borogroves,
 And the mome raths outgrabe.

*   *   *

- Make a list of compound words which could be grouped under one subject. Flip the words, as in "hoppergrass." Make a list poem. (See *Lists.*)

- Then choose one of the words as a point from which to leap. Call your piece "Gladesever," for instance.

- Mix up the parts of speech. Let verbs become nouns and nouns become adjectives. Let yourself be carried by the language. You can worry later about what it means.

- Imitate "The Jabberwocky." Give it a contemporary flair. Write about an encounter with a physical or metaphysical "Jabberwocky" of your own. Notice the meter and rhyme scheme which give the poem its shape and sound. Try to imitate this aspect as well: iambic tetrameter, with iambic trimeter in the last line of each stanza, and a rhyme scheme of abab. (See *The Weave of Meter.*)

- I read *Finnegan's Wake* in a reading group with many Joyce scholars and the help of a published skeleton key. But a first approach to Joyce's style might be to see how much sense can be gleaned from the sound. Read each sentence in the above passage aloud, and then paraphrase it without too much thought. In a workshop, it is fun to see the many different interpretations which result.

  (See *The Man-Moth, Versions of Translation,* and *Dream Logic.*)

Hearing the Dirt

Our language reveals the natural world—it is rich with metaphor. We "branch out" and "hear the dirt," without consciously associating the terms. And yet they are evidence that our daily lives are rich in metaphor. Poor dirt. It gets such a bad rap. Think of what gets labeled as "dirty" in our society. And yet dirt provides everything for us. It is the perfect metaphor for what we need and what we push out of our homes.

Try making a list of all the "natural" metaphors you can. Make a list of other metaphors—technological metaphors, for instance: plugged-in, wired, breakdown, interface. What do these say about the society in which we live and how language changes?

Occasionally, to wake a college class up, I have asked them to consider the terms we have for sexual activity in our culture. Are they reciprocal, non-reciprocal, violent? I have sent the students to the *Oxford English Dictionary* to look up "bad words." The subject is definitely worth talking about, and interestingly, to analyze and trace the origin of such words lessens their power. Such a discussion affords the opportunity to talk about the power that language can hold, and to consider the origins of all words. It also makes one think about the use of particular language within literature and how words and idioms (words or sayings peculiar to a language or region) might reflect deeper meaning.

Translation of an idiom can reveal startling connections. There is a German idiom my father often used when I asked too many questions: *"Kind, Du fragst mir Löcher im Bauch,"* which translates "Child, you ask me holes in my stomach." As I grew older, I could feel the weight of his memories as a child in WWII-era Germany reverberating within the phrase.

* * *

- The idioms of a language can offer great material. Make a list of idiomatic expressions in English (or other languages) which do not translate well. Write a story which contains the idiom in a significant way, perhaps as an embarrassing moment.

- Collect words that have always felt good on your tongue. Use them in your writing.

- Use the dictionary. Find the origins of words. You will find that abstract words derive from something material. "Spirit," for instance, means wind. Many words also evolved from the act involved. "Poem," for instance, comes from the Greek word, *poein*, meaning *to create*. Sometimes dictionary definitions themselves can be "found poems."

(See *The Man-Moth*.)

Going to the Source

On one of my trips to Central America, one young Panamanian boy, Miguel, was astounded to learn that toilet paper came from trees. He could not believe such a thing would be done. A little girl also disbelieved, insisting that toilet paper didn't come from trees, but from Panama City. The moment made me think of a comment which one of my first-year college students back home had made in response to a classroom discussion about deforestation: "I mean, it's not like we need plants to live."

Both instances were examples of how removed we are from the source of things and led into the following exercise:

* * *

• Trace something used in everyday life—an object, a meal, electricity, water—back to its source. (In a workshop, you could bring in pictures, or objects, such as a seemingly innocuous stuffed animal made in a third-world country, a hamburger, a glass of water). There can be an element of life-changing journalism in this experience, as you find your way to the factory, a site of child-labor, the slaughterhouse, the nuclear power plant, the polluted river or water source that must be treated.

(See *Time's Arrow* and *Writing the Currents.*)

Encounters

We have all had "encounters" with species other than our own. Some are, of course, more meaningful and life-changing than others. Alice Walker, in her essay, "Am I Blue," uses an encounter with a horse to reveal the parallels between the horse's ordeal and the experience of her ancestors in slavery. (See *A Convincing Story*.) Loren Eiseley's essay "Bird and the Machine" reflects the life-altering experience of a specimen collector who changes his life-work after he recognizes the deep bond his captured sparrow hawk has with his mate. After keeping the captured specimen overnight, Eiseley feels compelled to free him in the morning:

> He lay there a long minute without hope, unmoving, his eyes still fixed on that blue vault above him. It must have been that he was already so far away in heart that he never felt the release from my hand...In the next second after that long minute he was gone. Like a flicker of light, he had vanished...Then from far up somewhere a cry came ringing down.
> I was young then and had seen little of the world, but when I heard that cry my heart turned over. It was not the cry of the hawk I had captured; for, by shifting my position against the sun, I was now seeing farther up. Straight out of the sun's eye, where she must have been soaring restlessly above us for untold hours, hurtled his mate. And from far up, ringing from peak to peak of the summits over us, came a cry of such unutterable and ecstatic joy that it sounds down across the years and tingles among the cups of my quiet breakfast table.
> —Loren Eiseley (1907-1977)

Elizabeth Bishop's "The Fish" and "The Moose" are poems which reflect significant moments of connection to the natural world. In "The Fish," the speaker has caught a fish, who hasn't "fought at all," and as she sees the evidence of his past struggles, the old fish hooks "like medals with their ribbons/frayed and wavering/a five-haired beard of wisdom/trailing from his aching jaw," she has a moment of awakening, and lets the fish go.

In "The Moose," a long bus ride is interrupted by the sudden appearance of a moose on the road:

> A moose has come out of the impenetrable wood
> and stands there, looms, rather,
> in the middle of the road.
> It approaches; it sniffs at
> the bus's hot hood...

We have all had such encounters which opened our eyes further. Of course, experiences such as these may take awhile: months, years, even decades to work through our consciousness before we realize their significance in our lives.

Often, students who have told me that they never experienced any such "encounter" will have at least a small one within the week. Likely, this is because they have suddenly become differently attuned to their surroundings and are ready to have one. But it may not be a pretty one, or a sweet story. One person I know who has made the environment her lifework did so after killing a bird as a child. Another told me about having to "finish off" his sister's deer on a family hunting trip. He climbed on its back to slit its throat. The deer tried to stand and bucked as he killed it. He was covered with blood by the end of the procedure. He said he never hunted again.

William Stafford's "Traveling through the Dark" speaks of a troubling encounter with a deer killed by a car, and the difficult decision the speaker must make, when he feels the unborn fawn still alive inside her:

> I stood in the glare of the warm exhaust turning red;
> around our group I could hear the wilderness listen.
>
> I thought hard for us all my only swerving —
> then pushed her over the edge into the river.

*   *   *

- Write about an encounter in nature you have had which altered your perspective somewhat. Describe the encounter and the feelings it awakened in you. Sometimes an experience

which seemed minute at the time might awaken feelings
years later, as it reverberates over the years.

PAUL LAKE (b. 1951)

Blue Jay

A sound like a rusty pump beneath our window
Woke us at dawn. Drawing the curtains back,
We saw—through milky light, above the doghouse—
A blue jay lecturing a neighbor's cat
So fiercely that, at first, it seemed to wonder
When birds forgot the diplomacy of flight
And met, instead, each charge with a wild swoop,
Metallic cry, and angry thrust of beak.

Later we found the reason. Near the fence
Among the flowerless stalks of daffodils,
A weak piping of feathers. Too late now to go back
To nest again among the sheltering leaves.
And so, harrying the dog, routing the cat,
And taking sole possession of the yard,
The mother swooped all morning.

                              I found her there
Still fluttering round my head, still scattering
The troops of blackbirds, head cocked toward my car
As if it were some lurid animal,
When I returned from work. Still keeping faith.
As if what I had found by afternoon
Silent and still and hidden in tall grass
Might rise again above the fallen world;
As if the dead were not past mothering.

Dear Star, Do You Know the Moon?

As children, we asked a great many questions. And, sometimes, we got answers. Often, we got evasions, the reasons for which we may later have understood.

Our understanding of the physical world is based on observation and on the asking of questions based on what we see. Perhaps this questioning (and ordering) approach might have something to do with the rift between faith and science. Faith encourages us not to ask questions. Science demands that we do.

In interdisciplinary programs, when I have taken students to places such as the Everglades or Fairchild Tropical Gardens for field work, they were often asking questions for their science projects. There is a certain kind of question one asks in a scientific setting: "What specific nutrients does a certain kind of plant need? What predators keep a certain pest under control?"

But when they came to my class, they would ask a different kind of question, or sometimes, the same question in a different way: "Tree, why do you have those spikes?"

Joseph Campbell believed in addressing nature as "thou," that the direct, personal query became a different act entirely. William Blake, in "The Tyger," takes this kind of reverential approach:

WILLIAM BLAKE (1757-1827)

The Tyger

Tyger! Tyger! burning bright
In the forests of the night,
What immortal hand or eye
Dare frame thy fearful symmetry?

In what distant deeps or skies
Burnt the fire of thine eyes!
On what wings dare he aspire?
What the hand, dare seize the fire?

And what shoulder, & what art,
Could twist the sinews of thy heart?
And when thy heart began to beat,
What dread hand? & what dread feet?

What the hammer? what the chain,
In what furnace was thy brain?
What the anvil? what dread grasp,
Dare its deadly terrors clasp?

When the stars threw down their spears
And water'd heaven with their tears:
Did he smile his work to see?
Did he who made the Lamb make thee?

Tyger! Tyger! burning bright
In the forests of the night,
What immortal hand or eye
Dare frame thy fearful symmetry?

Even young children respond to Blake's poem. They all understand it on some level. They have all seen a cat's eyes burn or flash in the night. They all respond in some way to the mysteries of the universe.

Without fail, some students, especially younger ones, point out to me that "Tyger" is misspelled, which provides a nice opportunity to talk about how language changes over time.

I like to use Greg Brown's album of Blake's *Songs of Innocence and Experience* set to music when we read this poem. One hears the jungle and growl in Brown's rendition of "The Tyger." (See *Orchestrations.*) Some lines from Yeats' "Among School Children" provide another good example of this inquiry and raise new questions about the part and the whole, and what it is possible to know:

O chestnut tree, great-rooted blossomer,
Are you the leaf, the blossom, or the bole?
O body swayed to music, O brightening glance,
How can we know the dancer from the dance?
—William Butler Yeats (1865-1939)

When I ask students to try this, to ask questions of something in "nature," I am always surprised by the ingenuity of the questions and the choices of what to address. Invariably, they ask to widen the guidelines of the exercise: "Can we ask more than one thing?" "Do we have to ask something real?" "Can the 'nature' answer us?" They seem delighted to be allowed, and their approaches have opened the exercise up to new possibilities.

> Sun, what came first, dark or light?
> Moon, how do you shimmer?
> Stars, why do you come out at night?
> Moon, again, how does your shadow glimmer?
> Chelsea, dark came before.
> Chelsea, I'm not sure.
> Chelsea, we can't be seen in the day.
> Chelsea, I don't know what way.
> —Chelsea Roth, age 9

> O great rock that is the earth
> Tell me now of your awesome birth.
> Tell me now that I may know
> what happened here four billion years ago.
>
> O great sea upon the rock
> Tell me before my boat leaves dock
> What strange creatures do reside
> beneath your flowing, raging tide?
>
> O wide sky above the seas,
> tell me what I must know, please.
> As my aircraft does advance
> How wide is your great expanse?
>
> O vacuum beyond the sky so bleak,
> give me the answer that I seek
> of the worlds that, upon you, ride
> on which do living creatures hide?
>
> O universe, the All I see
> Give me now what my mind so needs.
> Release your secret, let it be freed.
> Where is your edge? Where does it lead?
> —Joseph Datko, age 12

Sometimes students have even further disregarded the parameters of an assignment, or rather, more loosely interpreted "nature." One asked questions of "letters":

> Letters, letters, listen letters,
> why do you tell me what to do?
> You tell me what you want to do.
> You tell me beautiful things and sad things too.
> —Adriana, 4th grade

Another, Sarah Rothenberg, 3rd grade, decided to query her TV:

> TV going on, why do you have so many channels?
> Why do you have Spanish when I am not Spanish?

I have used mostly examples from children in this chapter, but this is a good exercise for any age. Children may feel more comfortable asking questions. We often suppress that curiosity as we get older, perhaps because we fear seeming ignorant. Asking questions directly like this returns us, at least momentarily, to a state of innocence. It can re-awaken the awe we instinctively feel for the natural world, an awe which often gets forgotten in the daily grind of our lives.

*　*　*

• Ask questions of (or address) something in nature:

> Fig-tree, for such a long time I have found meaning
> In the way you almost completely omit your blossoms
> and urge your pure mystery, unproclaimed,
> into the early ripening fruit.
> Like the curved pipe of a fountain, your arching boughs drive
> the sap
> downward and up again: and almost without awakening
> it bursts out of sleep, into its sweetest achievement.
> Like the god stepping into the swan.
> —Rainer Maria Rilke, "The Sixth Elegy" (1875-1926)

• You could also incorporate meter into this exercise. Blake's "Tyger, Tyger" is an example of trochaic meter (stressed, unstressed). The excerpt from Yeats—"O Chestnut tree, great-rooted blossomer"—is iambic (unstressed, stressed).

Try writing your *apostrophes* (addresses) with trochaic or iambic meter. (See *The Weave of Meter.*)

(See also Donald Hall's "Names of Horses" in *Occasions for Reflection* and "apostrophe" in *How You Say a Thing.*)

Slowing the Speed of Light

As I write this chapter, the newspaper today has an article about scientists having discovered a way to slow the speed of light. Light, like sound, travels at different speeds through different things. Scientists have discovered that light will travel quite slowly through a very cooled gas—at about the speed of a swift bicyclist.

The discovery makes me think of the sounds I have heard while diving, how fast sound moves under water. In science classes, I was always the kind of student who wanted to know what the theory meant in a larger context. That connection has always felt like the spark of creativity. I know, instinctively, what this new discovery implies: as we get to very low temperatures, for instance, there is very little energy left for anything: mass, time, light. At very low temperatures, one cannot tell mass from time, or even one mass from another mass. Our entire existence is based on such distinctions, so our new ability to slow the speed of light holds radical implications. Science has always held this kind of fascination for me.

I remember first reading Walt Whitman's well-known poem, "When I Heard the Learned Astronomer." (See *Open Season*.) The speaker, looking at the "proofs, the figures...the charts and diagrams," becomes "tired and sick," and leaves the room to look silently up at the stars. I liked the moment of looking at the stars, but I also instinctively wanted to defend the science. I have heard poems within astronomers' lectures and taken them with me when I went out to look at the stars. The approaches can be complementary. But, granted, Whitman wrote the poem in 1865, a time when science was under the more immediate influence of a Cartesian mechanistic approach. Today's science is more open to the unknowable.

Sometimes I introduce a class to this poetry/science connection by asking a student for a chemistry or physics book. I open the book to a random page, run my finger down the text, and read what it lands on, as a "found poem."

A free radical which has lost an electron has an open bonding place and wants to bond with anything it can.

If Body A acts with a force on Body B, then Body B acts with a force of equal magnitude and opposite direction.

In scientific statements such as these, one hears echoes of so many other aspects of life. Some years ago, I came across an article by Richard Preston in *The New Yorker* about the Chudnovsky brothers solving for Pi. Pi goes on forever and can't be "calculated to perfect precision." Perhaps a deep design exists in the seeming "randomness." The article spoke about the way Pi is present in DNA, in a rainbow, in the pupil of an eye, in colors and music. Perhaps the answers to many questions are locked within the elusive number. The book *Gödel, Escher, Bach* helped me further recognize these connections, by articulating the parallels between math and art and music.

Finding connections like these in the world brings faith and science closer together. It makes us think about the tension between order and chaos. We hear the poetry inherent in this tension, in the physics of the universe. In these links, we find evidence of the deep design of the cosmos, the form in nature, of which we might be instinctively aware, but which perhaps, will always remain elusive.

* * *

- Try "finding" a poem in science. Choose something you previously considered purely scientific. You might simply deliver a chosen theory verbatim, or play with it in a new way. Perhaps juxtapose the theory with something non-scientific which it reminds you of.

- Strange scientific facts and new discoveries are at the core of most science fiction. Your local newspaper or magazines such as *Time* and *Newsweek* (or more specific science magazines, such as *Science* or *Nature*) can be a ready source of inspiration. Use a science item from one of these sources as the basis for a science fiction story or poem.

Earth Journey

Every so often in my classes, discussion turns to the topic of human versus geologic history. I have illustrated the timeline with a line across the whole blackboard, and a tiny mark at the end: this is when humans first appeared on the scene. Actually, on a blackboard scale, we would need a microscope to see the whole of human history. We are a continuation of the long earth story, of the universe story.

We are traveling from the moment of our conception, an incredible journey full of transformation. Joseph Campbell speaks of the "hero's adventure" which every person undergoes, the cycle of departure, fulfillment, and return. We cross thresholds which transform our consciousness. (See *Old Myth, New Myth*.)

The journey covers great distance. The journey itself is the story. Bruce Chatwin's *The Songlines* presents the aboriginal notion of the landscape and story being deeply connected. The aborigines walked the continent in the dreams, the songlines of their ancestors. Chatwin also traces how the movement itself, the walking, is deeply a part of our bodies. *Solvitur ambulando*. It is solved by walking.

We can find a peace through walking. I like to go for silent walks in the woods, silent even with others along. We walk together and find a new rhythm, a new way of being together. I get wonderful ideas when I walk, and when I run. I actually find myself working through poems in my head. It's a kind of meditation for me, to be silent and let my body take over. I often feel like writing after being silent for a while, gathering strength.

Many of us love to travel because things get simplified. When traveling, we leave much behind, everything but those "necessities" which can be compressed in the bags we carry. We can feel like we are entering a new world. Actually, we often are, but more importantly, we often enter a new state of consciousness, are more open to things, possibly because we have left the daily grind. Our senses become heightened.

When in the midst of other cultures, though, we can find ourselves linking things with our world back home. We instinctively find the parallels, the seemingly exotic rituals which correspond to something familiar. Drawing connections like these leads to further connections: our close proximity in the vastness of space, our genetic similarities that transcend cultural differences.

Thinking in geologic or subatomic terms helps us realize that we are deeply connected to the elements of the universe. Our bodies are about seventy percent water. We are made up of the same elements as stars. It is accurate and vital to think of ourselves as part of a greater web. These connections reveal themselves in our art, sometimes almost magically. Robert Bly says that "an ancient work of art such as *The Odyssey* has at its center a long floating leap, around which the poem's images gather themselves like steel shavings around a magnet." Our own journeys are part of an on-going story, deeply influenced by archetypal ideas.

The Odyssey, for example, the work itself, becomes a kind of center around which many other works of art gather. Perhaps it is the element of the dual journey which reaches us, the simultaneous inner and outer struggles. Norwegian anthropologist, Frederick Barthes, in his discussion of the Iranian nomads, the Basseri, observes that the journey itself is the ritual and that the raising and lowering of tents is a kind of prayer.

*   *   *

• Record your daily journey, urban or rural. Write often. Find the poetry in what might seem the mundane.

• Take a long walk through a place through which you would otherwise drive. Afterwards, record your observations. Trying to walk through suburbia or from one strip-mall to the next makes clear the way in which we have damaged our landscapes.

• Also walk in the places you still find beautiful—that street with all the banyan or live oak trees. Record what you see, in your mind rather than a photograph. Annie Dillard speaks of her own "shutter" opening when she walks without a camera.

- When you travel, keep a journal. Describe the places you visit. Focus on the landscape, the people, the language, the smells, the tastes. You might not complete any pieces about a place for years, but when you do return to it, either physically or in your writing, you'll be glad to have the record.

Writing from Culture

Nature includes culture, of course. Some of the exercises in this section speak to that tension and balance. Others encourage using music, art, science, and other languages to inspire and enhance your writing. Several chapters in other sections, *Storytelling and Myth-Making,* in particular, also involve accessing cultural and ancestral elements for your writing.

Alien Anthropology

A "newcomer" in a society has a unique perspective because of an unfamiliarity with certain linguistic and social conventions. He or she has to deduce meaning from what is observable. There is much we can learn by looking at familiar things with a new perspective. This naive view has the power to illuminate something obvious but hidden to most observers. Children, for instance, in their naiveté, are often the ones who reveal that the emperor has no clothes.

Writing from a perspective other than one's own can be mind-broadening. It is even more challenging to write about one's own culture through that other perspective. Our daily rituals, as common as they are to us, would seem bizarre to another culture, just as other cultures' rituals often strike us as strange. We have all opened *The National Geographic* and been fascinated by the "necks wound round and round with wire," as Elizabeth Bishop says in her poem, "In the Waiting Room." But how would our own daily rituals seem to an outsider—acts as common as shaving or applying make-up? What might other cultures think of plastic surgery? It is certainly no less bizarre than the scarification rituals of certain African tribes which shock us when we see them depicted in magazines or on television.

We have seen this use of an innocent perspective in mainstream media, in popular TV shows like *Third Rock from the Sun* or *The Wonder Years*, or in movies like *Crocodile Dundee* or *Look Who's Talking*. I have a favorite moment in the movie *Starman*, when the alien has observed and quickly assessed the rules of driving. He says, "I understand. Red means stop. Green means go. Yellow means go very very fast." He misunderstands the rules, but reveals a funny truth we all recognize.

It can be liberating to write from the "limited perspective" of an alien. Craig Raine's poem, "A Martian Sends a Postcard Home," is a good example, in its depiction of such common items as a clock and a phone:

> But time is tied to the wrist
> or kept in a box, ticking with impatience.
>
> In homes, a haunted apparatus sleeps,
> that snores when you pick it up.

> If the ghost cries, they carry it
> to their lips and soothe it to sleep
>
> with sounds. And yet, they wake it up
> deliberately, by tickling with a finger.

Raine's poem takes on various aspects of contemporary daily life, but it just touches the surface of possibility. Writing from an alien perspective is the type of exercise which will allow satire of many different aspects of human society. You could focus on a bar, a nuclear waste disposal site, a landfill, a school, a jail, a factory, a stripclub, a battlefield. It is a useful way to shake up your own notions about the society in which you live, to look at it with new eyes, the eyes of an outsider who may misunderstand, and, in doing so, reveal a deeper truth.

*   *   *

• Imitate Raine, and explore various aspects of twentieth century America through the perspective of an alien. Try writing a poem, like Raine's, or you might want to construct a narrative. Or you could even write it as an analytical piece, a report on your findings.

• The following is a variation on the above exercise, as it brings up the assumptions archaeologists make about past cultures. Imagine you arrive on a desolate, uninhabited Earth in some future year. Write through the perspective of an archaeologist, digging up the objects of our everyday lives. Focus on the symbolic value of the objects you find. What do they suggest about the culture which lived here? What assumptions can you make about a society which leaves behind the golden arches of *McDonalds* and a landfill full of styrofoam? What might a high heeled shoe, make-up, and a bikini say about the society? Write an assessment of some aspect(s) of twentieth century America based on the items that you find.

Writing the Currents

In a recent workshop, we spent quite a bit of time talking about the way writing has to take its time, how we might not be able to write in the center of an experience, how we might not yet have perspective on the issue. On the other hand, those are the times when it is often most important to write—to get the observations down on the page, although it may take years for any completed pieces to emerge. A workshop participant commented afterwards, "So journalists aren't really writers, since they have to produce writing in the moment?" The question surprised me. I had not intended that distinction.

As a journalist or columnist, one is required to write about events as they occur. There is hardly time for reflection. But often, the immediate associations the mind makes are the ones most true to our existence. The "angle" that initially reveals itself might actually be the one that survives. When we "report" or immediately respond to something, we also lay ground for future writing as well. Many journalists have gone on to write poems, stories, novels, memoirs or other types of reflective nonfiction about the events which they reported years ago.

It is a good idea to pay attention to current events and to notice where you are when they occur. Your own place in the scheme of things can sometimes be a vital detail, even if the situation merely drives home the reality of how removed you are—from the reality of war, for instance.

You might also find your subjects in other people's startling, or even disturbing, comments about current events. One university student in a workshop commented on the policy efficacy of the air strikes in Kosovo, because, as he put it, "Nobody is dying." What he meant was that no American soldiers were dying. But the statement reverberated in my head long after the class as evidence of our society's incredible distance from the reality of war.

Some issues speak to each of us, personally, more than others and move us to action, via the pen or through activism. Listen for your issues when they arrive. What you write about often has a direct link with your actions in the world and may lead you places you never might have expected.

* * *

• Keep a record in your journal of the events of the day (or week) and what they evoke in you. Remember, the basic reporting of today may very well be your stories of tomorrow.

• What news events do you remember most from your life? Do you remember where you were when you heard them? Write about your earliest memory of a news item.

The Man-Moth

I always liked the story of how Elizabeth Bishop got her inspiration for the poem, "The Man-Moth." The idea appeared to her as a misprint for "mammoth" in a newspaper. Typographical, grammatical, or foreign language translation errors can be great sources of inspiration. I have saved them for years, from various sources:

> — Sign in a Paris hotel elevator:
> *Please leave your values at the front desk.*

> — Answer on a high school science test:
> *H_2O is hot water. CO_2 is cold water.*

A student in one of my recent classes repeated the phrase, "as I lied in bed last night," several times in a writing assignment. I couldn't resist asking her in the margin to whom she was lying.

We have all made such blunders, particularly as we navigate other languages. On one trip to Colombia, a friend of mine, learning Spanish, thought she had learned how to say she was hungry. She kept rubbing her stomach, saying "Tengo mucho *hombre*," instead of the word for hunger, *hambre*. Unfortunately, she was actually telling some local women how "much man" she had. And I can remember more than one embarrassing moment of my own, where the situation got worse, as I discussed how *embarrasada* I was. Unfortunately, *embarrasada* means pregnant in Spanish.

But sometimes, the mistaken word can be most true. In the introduction of this book, for instance, I mention a conversation with an Emberá woman in Colombia, where I accidentally used the word *cajitas* (little boxes) to talk about my society's unfortunate methods of education. Modesta nodded, probably thinking I was speaking metaphorically.

Use these mishaps as leaping-off points. In *Leaping Poetry*, Robert Bly refers to the "long floating leap...from the conscious to the unconscious." Writing is very much about the accidental connection, and about allowing these to occur. I am reminded of Lawrence Ferlinghetti's poem about Chagall:

> Don't let that horse
> > eat that violin
> > cried Chagall's mother
> > > But he
> > kept right on
> > > painting...
> —Lawrence Ferlinghetti (b. 1919)

An important element in all good writing is the fresh, innovative *diction* (choice of word) and *syntax* (the arrangement of words). The source of the right word is one of those mysterious, elusive elements of writing. Sometimes, the right word arrives as a gift. Found poems and other serendipitous exercises help charge the imagination with new combinations.

(See *Hoppergrass* and *Versions of Translation*.)

* * *

- "Found poems": Try "finding" a poem in your belongings: the ingredients on a candy bar, the fine print on an ID, a page of your chemistry book, a funny or disturbing memo you received at work, an overheard conversation. (See *Eavesdropping*.) First, stick as close to the original as you can. You might find that you have an entire poem, or it might become the kernel of something more elaborate, perhaps an element of a story.

(See *Slowing the Speed of Light* or Nabokov's list in *Lists*.)

- "Random connections" is a fun exercise and a good game. Participants should break into sets of two. Without consulting each other, one should come up with a question: "Why?" The other should come up with a "Because." Some of the links work beautifully. Others are bizarre, but they might work even more beautifully. You could try this exercise with other links: if, then; I used to, but now. The following are several examples from students at Miami-Dade Community College:

Why do I see the things I see in your eyes?
Because the TV is on.

Why do we wear clothes?
Because we feel like dancing.

Why do I have to grow up?
Because you broke it.

Why is love so strong?
Because cows will always eat grass.

If I were a man
then the chains would be broken, and I would be free.

If I don't get to see *Star Wars* by the end of the week,
then the world will continue turning.

If frogs ruled the world,
then birds would swim.

I used to be afraid of the dark
But now I can't see a thing.

I used to fall in love at the drop of a pin.
But now I sleep with my eyes open.

I used to think my teachers weren't human.
But now I can drive.

- Refrigerator magnet words can be useful for sparking ideas (and you can use them while making dinner). Even self-proclaimed non-writers have found them inspiring. In a workshop, you could also use word lists or cards. Make a list or pile of nouns, verbs, adjectives, etc. and then pick from the piles to see what constructions result. You could select consciously, or you might close your eyes and pick randomly. It is rare, of course, that a whole poem or story will emerge from such serendipitous exercises, but perhaps a new image or idea will appear. I confess that occasionally a line from my refrigerator finds its way into a piece of writing.

(See also *Dream Logic* and *Completing Kubla Khan*.)

Lists

Several times in this book, I suggest making lists of words. Sometimes, the lists can be raw material for writing. Sometimes, the juxtaposition of words, like the inverted words in the chapter *Hoppergrass*, feel like they form a piece of their own.

We make lists every day, only some of which we write down. Lists can be useful in preparatory writing, because they let us see what we have to work with. They also help us organize and prioritize our thoughts. A list might work in or as a piece of writing because each item carries a symbolic weight. You can tell a great deal about a person through a list. A grocery list left in your buggy can be a found poem, or it might suggest a story. What people buy and what they throw away can be quite telling, I hate to admit. A friend once commented on someone's recycling bin, and now I always seem to notice people's recyclables on my morning walks in my neighborhood. Even something as mundane as a class list or a list of fabrics can be material. Julia Alvarez's (b. 1953) "Naming the Fabrics" uses a list of fabrics in a poem about her mother:

> ...in the gingham, calico, crepe and gauze,
> gabardine, organdy, wool, madras,
> selves, Mother, you've worn them all:
> jersey, chambray, satin, voile.

Vladimir Nabokov , in the novel *Lolita*, has Humbert Humbert come across a mimeographed list of names from Lolita's class (1899-1977). Humbert says of the list:

It is a poem I know already by heart.

> Angel, Grace
> Austin, Floyd
> Beale, Jack...
> Hamilton, Mary Rose
> Haze, Dolores
> Honeck, Rosaline...

A poem, a poem, forsooth! So strange and sweet was it to discover the "Haze, Dolores" (she!) in its special bower of names, with its bodyguard of roses—a fairy princess between her two maids of honor...The tender anonymity of this name with its formal veil ("Dolores") and that abstract transposition of first name and surname, which is like a pair of new gloves or a mask?

"Listing" can be a natural extension of many writing group discussions or personal encounters. About a year ago, we were talking in one of my workshops about our increasing reliance on technology. Some students claimed they didn't feel so reliant on devices. I asked them all to take a few minutes and list the machines they had already used that day. Their lists consisted of the obvious: phones, cars, computers, toasters, clocks, and the more individual: electric toothbrushes, hairdryers, beepers. As their lists filled their pages, the sheer number of their entries made the argument for me.

*　*　*

- Reflect on a seemingly mundane list in an "unexpected" way to make a point, as Nabokov does.

- Make a list of everything in the bathroom medicine cabinet, in the refrigerator, on your desk, etc. Or make a list of many types of one thing (such as Alvarez's fabrics). Develop a piece around this list.

- Make a list of items you would put in a time capsule, to best represent our era. The items you choose should probably symbolize specific aspects of our culture.

(See *Alien Anthropology* and *Bottle, Baseball, Bra*.)

Define the Color Blue

- Define a color, or something else which is not usually "defined." Or redefine something in a different way. It could be the simplest of ideas or emotions: home, or fear, for instance. Being asked to define them changes your approach. Mix imagery from different senses. (See "synesthesia" in *How You Say a Thing*.) Try to give tangible things an abstract quality and intangible things a concreteness.

- Address the color, as Federico Garcia Lorca addresses "Green" in this excerpt from "Sleepwalker's Ballad" (1899-1936):

> Green I love you green.
> Green of the wind. Green branches.
> The ship far out at sea.
> The horse above on the mountain.
> dark at her waist,
> she's dreaming there on her terrace,
> green of her cheek, green hair,
> with eyes like chilly silver.
> Green I love you green.
> Under the moon of the gypsies
> things are looking at her
> but she can't return their glances...

- If you find a question or a request in a piece that intrigues you, answer it, or respond to it.

Trees like Monstros

I had a dream I was afuera
and there were big arboles.
It look like el forest.
The trees look like monstros.
  —Dominique Flores, 3rd grade

Juxtaposing languages can have a powerful effect. Some words just fit the language. Living in Miami, one gets used to the constant merging of language—Spanglish is heard everywhere.

What is Language?

What es language
Ich ne sais pas
Maybe mucho mots
Pero aussi viele lettres
Où esta language
Je no know pas
En les bücher, ou
In los journaux
Mais in the end
Sprache esta dans
Our cerveau.
  —Carlos Anllo, UM

My Life Floating

Left my family
To search for a sueño.
I throw myself into el mar
With my strength my only salvacíon.
Dreams and deseos
Carry the raft into the ocean.
I'll be able to see mi papa
With the only thing I can give him.
  —Daniel Hernandez, UM

*   *   *

- Write a poem or story substituting certain words with their equivalent in another language. This probably works best if you are bilingual, but if you are not, you might think of the words you do know in another language. Why do you remember them? Is there a story behind the words or phrases—how they planted themselves in your brain? Use one of these words or phrases as the impetus for a piece. Some words struck me as extraordinarily memorable the first time I heard them, because of their musicality, their root, or their meaning. The Spanish *sueño* feels dream-like to me. I've always liked the French *plume* because of the feather and pen connection. *Besuchen*, German for visit, contains the word *suchen*, to seek.

    (See also "Bilingual/Bilingüe" in *Committing a Rhyme*.)

Versions of Translation

As Robert Frost once put it, poetry is "what gets lost in translation." With poetry, in particular, there are grand debates about such issues as fidelity to the meaning as well as to the music of the original poem. Some "translations" depart extensively and are referred to as *versions* instead.

* * *

• Find and examine several translations of a poem or piece of short prose. See which appeal more and try to identify the reasons. Is the imagery more startling? Is there more attention to rhythm? Try your own translation or version of the piece.

Beyond Versions

• Read a short piece of writing in a language you do not know and "translate" it according to the sound of the words and the meaning they suggest. Obviously, this process is unlikely to yield an actual translation, but it might spur on an interesting piece of writing.

• Take a well-known line of poetry or a famous sentence or passage (like the first sentence of *Moby Dick* or *The Gettysburg Address*). Identify the nouns. Look up each noun in the dictionary and replace it with the noun which follows in the dictionary. The replacement will likely yield a nonsense passage, but one which often contains interesting twists for a plot, or a new combination of sound:

Some years ago, having little or no money in my purse, I decided I would sail about a little and see the watery part of the world. (*Moby Dick*)

Some yearns ago, having little or no Mongols in my pursuit, I decided I would sail about a little and see the watery Parthenon of the Worm.

- "Translate" a famous passage into a different form of English. This exercise works well as a group activity and provides a good opportunity to talk about the importance of dialect. For instance, use the opening paragraph of Edgar Allen Poe's "The Tell-Tale Heart," and have the murderer use a different dialect: from the deep South, that of a Brooklyn youth, Spanglish, etc.

True!—nervous—very, very dreadfully nervous I had been and am; but why will you say that I am mad? The disease had sharpened my senses—not destroyed—not dulled them. Above all was the sense of hearing acute. I heard all things in the heaven and in the earth. I heard many things in hell. How, then, am I mad? Hearken! and observe how healthily—how calmly I can tell you the whole story.

It is impossible to say how first the idea entered my brain; but, once conceived, it haunted me day and night. Object there was none. Passion there was none. I loved the old man. He had never wronged me. He had never given me insult. For his gold I had no desire. I think it was his eye!—yes, it was this! He had the eye of a vulture—a pale blue eye, with a film over it. Whenever it fell upon me, my blood ran cold; and so, by degrees—very gradually—I made up my mind to take the life of the old man, and thus rid myself of the eye forever.

—Edgar Allan Poe (1809-1849)

Word!—nervous—I was mad scared, yo! But why you got to be say I'm trippin', you know? The disease woke me up—I ain't sleepin.' My ears was on fire with knowledge! I heard things in da' heaven above and da earth, and all the way down to Hell. How am I nuts? Peep this! 'Cuz I got a story to tell.

I don't know how it got in my head, yo, but once it was there, yo boom—it haunted me day and night. There was no beef, no hype, 'cuz I had mad love for the old geezer! I ain't got no reason, ain't got no rhyme. He never dissed me. I wasn't trying to take his paper. But he had this nasty ol' lookin' eye. He

had eyes like a vulture, blue, all glazed and all! Whenever he
peeped me, my blood ran cold, and so over time, I decided to
cap him before he got me.

(Michelle Bynum, Jeremy Goldsmith, Jennifer Pearson, UM)

You could, of course use any of many well-known works for this
exercise. The passage is a good, albeit eerie choice, because of the
urgent voice: the madman who tries to convince us of his sanity. It
also contains several archaic words such as *Hearken*, which offer
opportunity for humorous translations.

(See exercises in *Orchestrations* and *Sonnet.*)

Orchestrations

Music, of course, is a great source of inspiration and has been closely linked to literature throughout ages and cultures, such as the traditional ballads of Ireland or the operas and ballets which have set many great works of literature to music. In the oral tradition of ancient Greece, poetry was often set to music. The choruses of tragedies and comedies were sung, with or without instrumental music. This tradition in Greece continues to this day. A great many contemporary Greek musicians set famous ancient and modern poems to music. Many composers elsewhere do the same, though not to the same degree, perhaps.

Music in many ways enhances my own writing and teaching. I have found it useful to explore different angles on works of literature via contemporary versions, such as Greg Brown's rendition of Blake's *Songs of Innocence and Experience*. (See "The Tyger" in *Dear Star, Do You Know the Moon?*) I have also used Loreena McKennitt's renditions of folk songs and poems by such poets as Blake and Yeats to approach the poem from a different angle. Her reworking of Yeat's "The Stolen Child," in particular, found its way into my consciousness. Hearing the music repeatedly had something to do with the refrain "Come away, O human child!/To the waters and the wild" appearing in the center of one of my own poems.

Many contemporary musicians allude to works of literature. Dire Straits has an interesting "Romeo and Juliet," which gives the old story contemporary language:

> come up on different streets they both were streets of shame
> both dirty both mean yes and the dream was just the same...
> juliet the dice were loaded from the start...
> when you gonna realize it was just that the time was wrong juliet?

(See also *Old Myth, New Myth.*)

Many twentieth century songs use traditional forms, such as the ballads of Woody Guthrie and Bob Dylan. Nancy Griffith's rendition of Dylan's (b. 1941) "Boots of Spanish Leather" is a favorite of mine to use in workshops, because of its poignant closure. The song tells the story of a man going off to sea. He asks his love several times what gift he should bring her, but repeatedly, she just asks him to carry himself back to her "unspoiled," and continues in such a fashion:

> If I had the stars of the darkest night
> And the diamonds from the deepest ocean
> I'd forsake them all for your sweet kiss
> That's all I wish to be ownin'.

When she gets a letter from him, saying he doesn't know when he'll be coming back again, "depending on how [he's] feeling," she knows the score and in graceful, but practical resignation says:

> Take heed, take heed of the western wind
> Take heed of stormy weather
> And yes there is something you can send back to me
> Spanish boots of Spanish leather.

(See also *Ballads and Ballades.*)

Song, story and poetry are linked in the form of the ballad, which offers a good sense of the lineage in music. Tracing the influences on contemporary music can be an enlightening process: the fact that rock and roll emerged, for instance, out of rhythm and blues. (See *Crossroads.*)

Songs may be where people go to find their poetry, perhaps because of the artificial distinctions between poetry and song in our culture. In truth, the two are more linked than it would sometimes appear.

* * *

• Listen to poems you know which have been set to music. See what emerges beneath your pen during or after. Do you feel differently about the poem after you hear it sung?

106

- Listen to your favorite songs (rock, rap, country, hip-hop, etc.) with the intention of freewriting afterwards. Use the song as a leaping-off point. Perhaps use a line as an epigraph.

- Imitate the rhythm of different kinds of music with your lines or sentences. Let the meter of your lines or sentences reflect the influence of the beat. (See *The Weave of Meter.*)

- Listen to songs in a language you don't know. Can you tell the tone of the song—longing, joy, reverence? "Translate" the song via the tone. (See *Versions of Translation.*)

- Listen to classical music. Try writing as you listen. Try Beethoven's Sixth Symphony, for instance, the "Storm Passage," created by violins and cellos. (If you introduce it to others who do not know the piece, you might withhold the name, at first, to see what kind of "stormy" feelings get evoked and appear beneath the pen.)

- Loreena McKennitt may have chosen to set "The Stolen Child" to music because of the refrain, which made it a natural candidate. Try writing a poem with a refrain.

WILLIAM BUTLER YEATS (1865-1939)

The Stolen Child

Where dips the rocky highland
Of Sleuth Wood in the lake,
There lies a leafy island
Where flapping herons wake
The drowsy water-rats;
There we've hid our fairy vats,
Full of berries
And of reddest stolen cherries.
Come away, O human child!
To the waters and the wild

With a faery hand in hand,
For the world's more full of weeping than you
    can understand.

Where the wave of moonlight glosses
The dim grey sands with light,
Far off by furthest Rosses
We foot it all the night,
Weaving olden dances,
Mingling hands and mingling glances
Till the moon has taken flight;
To and fro we leap
And chase the frothy bubbles,
While the world is full of troubles
And is anxious in its sleep.
Come away, O human child!
To the waters and the wild
With a faery hand in hand,
For the world's more full of weeping than you
    can understand.

Where the wandering water gushes
From the hills above Glen-Car,
In pools among the rushes
That scarce could bathe a star,
We seek for slumbering trout
And whispering in their ears
Give them unquiet dreams;
Leaning softly out
From ferns that drop their tears
Over the young streams.
Come away, O human child!
To the waters and the wild
With a faery hand in hand,
For the world's more full of weeping than you
    can understand.

Away with us he's going,
The solemn-eyed:
He'll hear no more the lowing

Of the calves on the warm hillside
Or the kettle on the hob
Sing peace into his breast,
Or see the brown mice bob
Round and round the oatmeal-chest.
For he comes, the human child,
To the waters and the wild
With a faery hand in hand,
From a world more full of weeping than you
      can understand.

Stage Directions

Films offer some valuable lessons for writing, when seen with a particular kind of vision. Pay attention to the cross-cutting (simultaneous action) and to the way the filmmaker makes the transition from one scene to the next. This type of attention is essential if you aspire to filmmaking or screenwriting, of course, but it can also be highly inspiring for other kinds of writing.

One of the features of Robert McDowell's (b.1953) long narrative poem in blank verse, *The Diviners*, for instance, is the quick change in scenes, reminiscent of movie cuts. The shifts and juxtapositions speed up the pace of the action:

> Tom:
>
> The screen door slams. I lock my door again.
> I study notes and pull out all my books
> On polar exploration; I memorize
> The characters, events, all dates and charts.
> I prepare for when I'm older, more important,
> Maybe President. Or I may leave.
> It must be cold outside the galaxy,
> But knowing about Admiral Scott will help.
>
> Al slams his office door. He works the phone,
> And says hello as he loosens the knot of his tie.

One film I have used in both creative writing and writing about ecology courses is *Koyaanisquatsi* (a Hopi word for "Life out of Balance"). The film is wordless—or rather, it has one word: *Koyaanisquatsi*. It tells the story (via images and the juxtaposition of them) of the effect of humans on the natural world and depicts the disconnected and frenetic pace of our modern lives. Sped up images from the assembly lines of a sausage factory are followed by humans pouring up escalators and filling and emptying congested subway stations.

110

* * *

- Try giving words to the juxtapositions you see in certain films. Describe scenes. It is a good idea to do this shortly after you have seen the film, while it is fresh in your memory. You might just freewrite in your journal as material for later.

- Write "stage directions" for a character as a short prose piece or as a poem:

Note to Actress 1

Enter wearing black
capri pants and tiger-print
tube-top, cleavage calling
men against the bar.
Light up when their eyes
turn to the butterfly barrette
opening its wings in your yellow hair.
Sit down and smile.
The tall one crosses the stage
to buy you a Chardonnay.
Talk with your eyes. Look away,
quickly looking back.
Exit with the tall one,
your company for the night
reassigned.
          —Vivian Fel, UM

Art Speaks

Try writing from art. Carry your journal with you to museums. Whenever I leave an exhibit, I usually have one or two pieces which leave with me (in my consciousness, I mean, or maybe as postcards). Wandering through a gallery usually fills you with rich images and inspiration.

In a workshop one semester, for instance, we were talking about the symbolism of horses in our culture and in literature. The Lowe Art Museum in Miami had an exhibit of Deborah Butterfield's horses—huge sculptures made of scrap metal, containing items such as tricycles for innards. We took a "field trip," and each participant chose a piece to use as inspiration for a writing exercise.

Many writers have responded to pieces of art. You have abundant models to follow: Randall Jarrell's "The Knight, Death, and the Devil" after Albrecht Dürer's painting; Anne Sexton's "The Starry Night," after Van Gogh; Lawrence Ferlinghetti's "Don't Let that Horse Eat that Violin," after Marc Chagall; W.H. Auden's "Musée des Beaux Arts," where he considers Brueghel's "Landscape with the Fall of Icarus"; Donald Hall's "The Scream," after Edward Munch, to name a few.

* * *

• Write a response to a piece of art. You could use images in a book or you might decide to write directly after visiting an exhibit.

• Give someone a voice: a figure in a sculpture or painting.

• Riff on the art. What does the painting make you think about? Where does it send you?

• Write a piece which focuses on a seemingly obscure detail in the piece of art—a cat on the windowsill in the background, for instance.

Dream Logic

Poetry is when your
bed flips over and you're at the sea
and your bed begins
to float on the air like it is
flying
        — Jesse Feldmann, 3rd grade

Dreams suspend reality and can be a great source of inspiration for writing. They tap the elements of our unconscious and can synthesize things in a way our conscious logic will not allow. When we dream, we are ladling out of a universal soup pot, which is why we all have dreams that are variations on certain themes. Who hasn't dreamt of falling, for instance? Mythologist Joseph Campbell's explanation for this universality draws on Carl Jung's idea that dreams and myths arise from our collective unconscious and give form to archetypal ideas. (See *Old Myth, New Myth.*)

The dream world is a surreal one, with its fantastic and incongruous imagery. A body of art has arisen out of this tradition. The Dadaist movement formed during the first World War, in response to the insanity created by the self-proclaimed "logical" world. The approach was an attempt to shock the world out of its terrible traditions. Surrealism emerged from Dadaism in 1922, first as a literary movement. Surrealism promoted releasing the fantastic, dream-like creations of the unconscious. The movement professed spontaneity and depiction of the process of the mind, rather than craft as the essential element in literature. However, the reality is that most surrealist art was not at all spontaneous. Andre Bretón, for instance, spent six months on a poem of thirty words, in order to achieve what looked like spontaneity. And many surrealist visual artists would do several versions of the same "automatic drawing" in pursuit of such an effect of "immediacy."

Many writers outside the surrealist movement have drawn inspiration from the surreality of dreams. Samuel Taylor Coleridge, for instance, claims that "Kubla Khan" in its entirety came to him in

a vision during a dream. (See *Completing Kubla Khan.*)
And many poems and stories have a dream-like fog about them, with surreal visitations, such as Federico Garcia Lorca's poem "Sleepwalker's Ballad" (see *Define the Color Blue*) Wallace Stevens' poem, "A Rabbit as King of the Ghosts", Nikolai Gogol's story "The Nose", or Franz Kafka's story "The Metamorphosis."

Dali's paintings are an example of surrealist painting which many will recognize. Contrary to much modern painting, Dali's titles (for example, *Three Surrealist Women Holding in Their Arms the Skins of an Orchestra*) are an integral part of his art. This painting is a good example of surrealist imagery. The three women are clearly women, but their heads are blooming flowers, instead of faces. The setting is a beach, and they are holding fluid instruments in their arms. All of the images are painted realistically, but are placed in incongruous settings, with startling juxtapositions. In another of my favorites, "Archaeological Reminiscence of Millet's *Angelus*," Dali re-paints Millet's male and female figures as archaeological ruins.

Nature itself is often surreal, with its strange combinations and creations. However, just as in nature, where both order and chaos exist together, art must contain elements of both the logical and the irrational. A balance is necessary, or the irrational can actually become tedious. As Frederick Turner says in *Natural Classicism*, the mind can become as "habituated to meaningless flux as to mindless regularity."

All writers use a measure of surrealism, whether they consider themselves "surrealists" or not. Metaphor, in its very foundation, often has a surreal quality about it—one thing becomes something else, as in the following excerpt from Michael Hettich's "Mercy, Mercy":

> Every time we argue
> my wife becomes a horse.
> Not a symbol or a dream.
> A horse. There's nothing
> I can do then but let her
> run.
>
> On her back I can hardly
> breathe. I am ducking
> branches and wires
> as she races down the street...

Consider the powerful effect of denying symbol and dream in the above lines. In similar fashion, Gabriel Garcia Marquez, considered the quintessential writer of magic realism, claims that he made nothing up in his work—he just wrote down what the people told him. Magic realism is a literary movement distinct from surrealism, but also uses elements of the real and the unreal and often employs a kind of dream logic. The origin of the term is disputed, but is often thought to have originated from Cuban novelist Alejo Carpentiers' question: "What is the story of Latin America if not a chronicle of the marvelous in the real (*lo real maravilloso*)?" The term came to refer to the implausible, fantastic fiction which emerged in South America after World War II and includes such writers as Miguel Angel Asturias, Mario Vargas Llosa, and Laura Esquivel. Gabriel Garcia Marquez's *One Hundred Years of Solitude* is often considered the quintessential work of magic realism. Real historical events and depictions are merged with sudden "magical" moments, such as a woman visibly ascending to the heavens. Roots and branches of magic realism are seen in works by writers of other cultures such as Czech Franz Kafka (1883-1924) and more contemporary writers such as Czech novelist Milan Kundera, Italian novelist Italo Calvino, and novelist Robert Antoni, of Trinidadian heritage, to name a few.

* * *

• Harvest your dreams. Record them. Keep your journal or a separate dream journal beside the bed. A description of a dream might work as a piece on its own—or it might provide an interesting image or motif for a later work.

• Explore nursery rhymes and songs. Many have a surreal quality—like "Rock-a-Bye-Baby," for instance, or "Hey Diddle Diddle." Write a nursery rhyme. Or "translate" a nursery rhyme, like "Little Miss Muffet" (perhaps make it more contemporary). In a workshop, each participant might use the one they most clearly remember. The following is the beginning of a translation of "Hey Diddle Diddle" I wrote as an exercise years ago:

Hey spin spin,
the feline and the violin

It didn't survive as a poem, but the words reappeared later as the last lines of a poem:

> Last laugh, last carafe. Spin bottle spin.
> Hey diddle diddle. Feline. Violin.

(See Old Myth, New Myth and Versions of Translation.)

• The following is a derivation of a favorite exercise used by the surrealists, who enjoyed such collaborative, "random" exercises to produce writing. It was named Cadavre Exquis (Exquisite Corpse) from one of the lines which resulted: "The Exquisite Corpse Drinks New Wine." Because the exercise uses the logic of syntax, however, it will produce some coherency amidst the random connections.

As an exercise on your own, you could fill in the blanks as quickly as possible, without giving clear coherency from line to line, and see what results. Or, you could make the results even more random. In a workshop, everyone begin by filling in the blanks of the first line (try to make the individual line make sense), then pass it to the right. Each person then write the second line and pass it to the right, and so on. When all the lines are completed, read the results in your hands aloud. (For even more surreal results, you could fold down each line before you pass it.)

At dawn, the __sound adjective__ __noun, type of machine__
began to __verb__ __adverb__
next to the __color adjective__ __noun,place__ .
The __smell adjective__ __noun, animal__
__verb (past tense)__ __adverb__
on the __texture adjective__ __noun, piece of furniture__ .
Later that morning, the __emotional adjective__ __noun, musical instrument__
__verb(past tense)__ __adverb__

through the __taste adjective__ __noun element of landscape__ .
This caused the _____.

Example:

At dawn, the noisy dishwasher
began to chuckle hysterically
next to the blue house.
The rancid cat
complained loudly
on the soft couch.
Later that morning, the sad piano
howled ferociously
through the bitter mountains.
This caused the windows to break.

(See *The Man-Moth* for additional exercises using random connections.)

• Become familiar with magic realism. We might take a cue from Marquez and listen for the "magically real" in our everyday lives and lineage. In other words, write down what people tell you. Look for the "magically real" in everyday life. Consider an image such as the following in Laura Esquivel's novel *Like Water for Chocolate:*

> The way Nacha told it, Tita was literally washed into this world on a great tide of tears that spilled over the edge of the table and flooded across the kitchen floor.
> That afternoon, when the uproar had subsided and the water had been dried up by the sun, Nacha swept up the residue the tears had left on the red stone floor. There was enough salt to fill a ten-pound sack—it was used for cooking and lasted a long time. Thanks to her unusual birth, Tita felt a deep love for the kitchen, where she spent most of her life from the day she was born.

Write an image such as "Tears flooded the room," and then elaborate on the image as a real occurrence. Tell your story convincingly (Take another cue from Marquez, who also has said that "you can get people to believe anything if you tell it convincingly enough.")

Completing Kubla Khan

"Kubla Khan, Or A Vision in a Dream. A Fragment" is Samuel Taylor Coleridge's famous fifty-four-line fragment. In a prefatory note to the poem, Coleridge explains that an entire poem (200-300 lines) appeared to him in a dream. In ill health, he had fallen asleep after taking a painkiller (likely laudanum). He was reading *Purchas His Pilgrimage*, likely the following sentences: "Here the Kubla Khan commanded a palace to be built, and a stately garden thereunto. And thus ten miles of fertile ground were inclosed with a wall." He believed he composed the entire poem in his sleep, but adds: "if that indeed can be called composition in which all the images rose up before him as *things*, with a parallel production of the correspondent expressions, without any sensation or consciousness of effort." On waking, he began to write down what he remembered. He was interrupted, however, by a person on business who took him away from the poem for more than an hour. When he returned to his room, Coleridge found that the rest of the poem had escaped his memory .

Like other Romantics, Coleridge believed writing to be an "organic" rather than a mechanical act. He rejected the notion of a work of art as being "mechanically" contrived to please a certain audience, for instance. He spoke of art as a living entity, growing and developing as one. This philosophy may have had something to do with his refusal to finish the fragment, which he felt had come to an unfortunate, untimely end. Or the fragment may, indeed, have been a fiction, meant to represent the subconscious and the organic nature of art. Because conflicting accounts from Coleridge himself exist, the circumstances surrounding the poem remain somewhat mysterious.

One can certainly relate to the notion of the interrupted process or idea, though our accounts may not be as dramatic as Coleridge's loss of two hundred composed lines. (See *Writing for Your Life*.) Many poets have since attempted to complete the famous fragment.

SAMUEL TAYLOR COLERIDGE (1772-1834)

Kubla Khan
Or a Vision in a Dream. A Fragment

In Xanadu did Kubla Khan
A stately pleasure dome decree:
Where Alph, the sacred river, ran
Through caverns measureless to man
    Down to a sunless sea.
So twice five miles of fertile ground
With walls and towers were girdled round:
And there were gardens bright with sinuous rills.
Where blossomed many an incense-bearing tree;
And here were forests ancient as the hills.
Enfolding sunny spots of greenery.

But oh! that deep romantic chasm which slanted
Down the green hill athwart a cedarn cover!
A savage place! as holy and enchanted
As e'er beneath a waning moon was haunted
By woman wailing for her demon lover!
And from this chasm, with ceaseless turmoil seething,
As if this earth in fast thick pants were breathing,
A mighty fountain momently was forced:
Amid whose swift half-intermitted burst
Huge fragments vaulted like rebounding hail.
Or chaffy grain beneath the thresher's flail:
And 'mid these dancing rocks at once and ever
It flung up momently the sacred river.
Five miles meandering with a mazy motion
Through wood and dale the sacred river ran,
Then reached the caverns measureless to man,
And sank in tumult to a lifeless ocean:
And 'mid this tumult Kubla heard from far
Ancestral voices prophesying war!

The shadow of the dome of pleasure
Floated midway on the waves;
Where was heard the mingled measure
From the fountains and the caves.
It was a miracle of rare device,
A sunny pleasure dome with caves of ice!

A damsel with a dulcimer
In a vision once I saw
It was an Abyssinian maid,
And on her dulcimer she played,
Singing of Mount Abora
Could I revive within me
Her symphony and song,
To such a deep delight 'twould win me
That with music loud and long
I would build that dome in air,
That sunny dome! those caves of ice!
And all who heard should see them there.
And all should cry Beware! Beware!
His flashing eyes, his floating hair!
Weave a circle round him thrice,
And close your eyes with holy dread,
For he on honey-dew hath fed,
And drunk the milk of Paradise.

(The Khan is a reference to the first khan, or ruler of the Mongol dynasty in 13th–century China. The named places are fictitious, as is the topography.)

*   *   *

• Though you might endeavor to complete the poem on your own, you could also try writing a collaborative closure:

In a group, read the poem aloud.

Notice how Coleridge uses rhyme, though not in a recurring pattern. The poem also has a generally iambic beat. Sometimes the line has five beats, sometimes four. (See *The Weave of Meter* and *Committing a Rhyme*.)

After noting such elements, read the poem aloud again (to get back into the rhythm).

Each person should write the next line of the poem, keeping in mind the general iambic beat and changing rhyme scheme. Don't give the meaning of the line too much thought, but allow the unconscious to take over somewhat. Try to "catch" the rhythm. (Take only about a minute or two per line) and then pass the papers to the right.

Each person then writes a second line, and passes the paper. This continues until the papers have traveled around the room, and you have the one which you began.

Complete the poem with your own final line. Read a few of them aloud.

(See also *Dream Logic.*)

Eavesdropping

My mother always told me, "Eavesdroppers never hear well of themselves." I believe it. So I try not to eavesdrop, at least not around people I know. But we all have a natural curiosity about other people's lives. If we didn't, storytelling would have no place in our world. Tuning into other people's lives, particularly in places where we are anonymous, can offer inspiration. Of course, many people today eavesdrop on chatrooms on the Internet, which can be an interesting experience in itself. But people don't tend to tell elaborate stories on the Internet, and there is something about the over*heard* story that can give a richness and reality to your listening and, later, to your writing.

Eavesdropping—the word itself is like a poem, like the words dropping magically from the eaves into your own writing.

* * *

• Here is your license to eavesdrop. Go to a public space (a café on the beach, bus, train, anyplace where you might mingle with people from many walks of life). Give yourself different "listening" exercises. Try to catch some dialogue, intonation. Transcribe the actual words they say.

> ...Hallelujahs mask oh-no-she-didn'ts...
> She didn't invite who to the wedding?
> Guess who's not invited to the mother's banquet.
> Deacon Wiley's sleeping with who?
> No wonder she hasn't been to choir practice...
> Sister Jones is testifying once again
> Going on about how the Lord brought her a Lexus.
> —Michelle Bynum, UM

• Use the eavesdropping to create a *dramatic monologue*. Let the character's speech create a dramatic scene. (See *Inhabitation*.)

Spells, Prophecies, and Prayers

When we think of a spell, we think of magic enacted to cause some kind of change. Language has tremendous power. The "spelling" of words has at its root this history of the realization of the transforming possibilities of language. The power of words is inherent in the "good books" of our religions: "In the beginning was the word..."

Our "spells" and rituals might work because of the way they function on a symbolic level. The object or action becomes symbolic of the intention. Our whole lives involve an elaborate matrix of symbols. Our daily and religious rituals certainly involve symbolic actions. When my Cuban Catholic friends put a cup of water to St. Clara in the window for clear thoughts on the day of a test, the symbolism is obvious. We also have less positive symbolic actions, like ripping up a love letter (or burning everything he or she ever gave you), which usually involve far more than the things destroyed.

Some years ago, a Colombian friend of mine suggested I "freeze" someone who was bothering me deeply. We wrote the name on a piece of paper bag, put it in a glass of water and froze it. I participated mostly for show, but the action actually did help me clear my thoughts of the person. It "froze" his effect on me. Such rituals have a distinct power on our consciousness, on our reactions to things.

A particular image or occurrence in our lives can sometimes have the effect of a spell on our writing—and loosen our tongues. And the writing itself might extend that magic and cause further things to come into being. A spell, in this way, might bring together prophecy and prayer. Wishing can have powerful consequences, perhaps because wishing something often compels us to bring about our desires. The articulation of what we truly want can be a major step in a shift in consciousness.

The language we use is a part of that "spelling." The *abracadabra* so often associated with spells, for instance, is believed to have been derived from Aramaic, the language of the Bible. It means "I hurl my thunderbolt."

*   *   *

• Write a piece which has a prophetic nature. For instance, write your own prophecy or horoscope for what the day, or month or year will bring.

• Write a piece which includes a ritual. Robinson Jeffers' "Return" always felt like a prayer or a spell to me:

> I will go down to the lovely Sur Rivers
> And dip my arms in them up to the shoulders.
> I will find my accounting where the alder leaf quivers
> In the ocean wind over the river boulders...
> — Robinson Jeffers (1887-1962)

• Write a spell for a character in a story to enact (like the witches in *Macbeth*). This is one way to distance the spell's energy from yourself.

• **Spells and Trochaic Meter**

When we think of the incantation which accompanies "traditional" spells, we think of an hypnotic arrangement, containing rhyme and meter. In Shakespeare's *Macbeth*, when the witches cast their well-known spell, the blank verse of the play changes to trochaic meter (a pattern of stressed, unstressed syllables) with rhyme and a repetition of sounds to heighten the effect of the magic. The word derives from the Greek *trochos*, meaning wheel. Trochaic meter has a kind of forward-skipping effect, and is a particularly effective meter for creating an "hypnotic" effect. (See *The Weave of Meter.*)

> Eye of newt, and toe of frog,
> Wool of bat, and tongue of dog,
> Adder's fork, and blindworm's sting,
> Lizard's leg, and howlet's wing —
> For a charm of pow'rful trouble.

Like a hell-broth boil and bubble.
Double, double, toil and trouble,
Fire burn and cauldron bubble.

• Write an emulation of the above spell. List the necessary ingre-
   dients in the first four lines (try using ingredients of this
   day and age). The choice of ingredients can also be a good
   way to talk about symbol. The items used in the spell
   could be chosen for their symbolic purpose: a love letter, a
   test, a dress, eye of newt? (hopefully not). List the
   elements and procedures for the spell as a kind of recipe.
   Laura Esquivel's novel, *Like Water for Chocolate* has this
   "magically real" element of symbolic food bringing about
   certain events. (See *Dream Logic.*)

   In the second half, include an incantation (with words
   such as "double, double, toil and trouble...") and the intent
   of the spell.

   Use trochaic meter throughout the spell.

   One caution: When I use this exercise in classes, I like to
   suggest that students frame their wishes in the positive
   (for obvious reasons). For instance, if you want to get
   someone out of your life, try a spell for something positive
   which will take the person far far away from you.

Wandering the Library

Libraries have become, in many ways, quite computerized affairs. On the one hand, it makes for faster searches, but on the other, it can also create the unfortunate impression that one need not come in contact with books.

Browsing in a library can lead you to unexpected places. It can be exciting to hold certain books in your hands, particularly an older book or a first edition by a favorite writer. I first experienced "special collections" at Brown University. The John Hay Library houses the Harris Collection, the largest collection of American poetry and plays.

At Brown, I often had my students visit the John Hay Library and look at first editions by poets we were reading in class: a first edition of *A Boy's Life*, with a poem inscribed by Robert Frost, for instance, or first editions of poets such as W.H. Auden, Emily Dickinson, and Wallace Stevens. I have since often included a visit to special collections as part of my workshops. It offers a different experience of books, and awakens a new appreciation of them.

I tell my students to wander the stacks, then write about an experience in the library. Charles Simic's poem, "In the Library," is a good example. The speaker in that poem comes across a dictionary of angels, "once as plentiful/As species of flies." Now they are "huddled in dark, unopened books." Timothy Steele's "The Library" is another good example—a reflection of closing time. Randall Jarrell's "A Girl in a Library" and "Children Selecting Books in a Library" are philosophical journeys which initiate from observations of people who are there.

* * *

• Wander a library. Bookstores are another option, obviously, particularly small fine bookstores, but the stacks of a library might offer a somewhat different experience. (Unfortunately, you can't wander the special collections of libraries without special permission, but you can wander the catalogues or find out what might be available.) Write about a particular book that catches your attention. Why does it draw you? Describe it. What does it evoke?

• Reflect on something that happens at the library. Even if it feels like nothing happens, make an everyday occurrence rich with language. (See the excerpt from Timothy Steele in *Stanzas.*)

• Reflect on someone you observe at the library. (Use the cautions from the chapter *Eavesdropping* and try not to make your observations too obvious.)

Perhaps allow your observations to lead into a philosophical comment, as Randall Jarrell does in the following excerpt from "Children Selecting Books in a Library":

Their tales are full of sorcerers and ogres
Because their lives are: the capricious infinite
That, like parents, no one has yet escaped
Except by luck or magic...
Read meanwhile...find one cure for Everychild's diseases
Beginning: Once upon a time there was
A wolf that fed, a mouse that warned, a bear that rode
A boy...

Writing with Form

An Introduction to Form

What do we mean by the term *form* in writing? It has been used to refer to the genre (epic, short story, novel, etc.); the structure of a work within a genre (ie: Shakespearian sonnet, one-act play); or many other arrangements or division of parts in writing. The purpose of this section is to address different aspects of form in writing, particularly poetry. The first few chapters deal with such questions as finding the genre of a piece, translating from one genre to another, and focusing on various components of writing, such as the grammar and rhythm of sentences.

The later chapters focus mostly on *closed form* in poetry, the term referring to the regular arrangement of stanza, meter, rhyme, or repetition. *Open form*, or free verse (poetry with no consistent pattern of meter or rhyme), is discussed specifically in *Open Season*. Many of the chapters in the other sections of the book can be used to inspire and address essential elements of both formal and free verse poems. Working in form can help to train your ear and can have the effect of making your free verse and prose more lyrical and rhythmical.

The later chapters also present examples of several specific *fixed poetic forms*, such as the sonnet and the sestina. Practicing each form is a kind of exercise in itself, because of the framework the rules for the form provide. You will find that following these rules can actually be quite liberating at times—it can often bring you to a place in your stream of consciousness which you might not otherwise have found. Structure, in a way, can enable freedom, just as grammar allows us to communicate. Attempting these exercises will also shed light on great poems of history written in these forms. And being familiar with them gives you additional tools for your own writing. Writing a villanelle or triolet, for instance, can hone the skill of using a repeated line or refrain. Once you have a good grasp of the form, you can use its influence to your best advantage—either by using the form itself or using it as inspiration for your own variations. When you find a form which particularly suits or intrigues you, search out its more elaborate history and the many examples in literature. It is also vital to note, however, that a competent exercise in a particular form is not necessarily a great poem. As I have mentioned several times in the book, we must keep in mind that the source of true art remains on many levels an enigma.

This section is not meant to offer a complete overview of form, but to offer the basics and some innovative suggestions, as a means to propel your writing forward and to exercise your aural and oral abilities. Remember, also, that it may take awhile for a subject to discover its true shape. Form should have meaning and purpose in a particular piece and find its subject organically. Writers spend decades, sometimes, working on a single short poem. It is a good idea to think of much of your writing as "exercise." It takes the pressure off, opens up the field to many possibilities. It keeps you going.

Genre to Genre

You will often find your genre as you write. You may not know if something is a poem, an essay, a play, a short story, or a novel until you are writing it. Many writers have cast and then re-cast their subjects in many different forms.

Shifting genre can reveal layers which remained hidden before. There are intensities which can be brought forth by a poem, just as there are details and dialogue which can be much more fully explored in prose. Sometimes, different genres might exist together in a single work.

Fred D'Aguiar's novel, *The Longest Memory*, for instance, has an innovative form. The book is a mosaic of the different voices of several characters, revealed via prose, poetry, diary entries, even editorials. Anthony Walton's nonfiction book, *Mississippi*, also breaks down genre delineation and uses such elements as personal testimony, essay, historical documents, and poetry to illuminate history and lineage. Michael Ondaatje's *The Collected Works of Billy the Kid* and *Coming Through Slaughter* each fuse history and legend in a series of poems and prose pieces which explore the lives of Billy the Kid and jazz legend Buddy Bolden, respectively. All three authors are poets whose prose seems deeply influenced by a poet's sense of rhythm and juxtaposition.

* * *

- You might take a well-known work and pay tribute by re-casting the same piece in a different genre. Write a letter or a poem, for instance, which contains an element of a play or story.

- Take a piece of your own writing and change its genre. Write the story as a poem, the poem as a dramatic scene, the dramatic scene as a letter, etc.

- Try writing about related subjects using different genres. You may find that a series of voices and/or approaches begins to emerge which might form a larger piece. Creating such a collage might also inspire different ways of handling voices.

(See *The Skeletons in Our Stories*.)

Vignettes

We all tell anecdotes of our lives, and jokes. The vignette is this type of form—short prose, complete on its own, but often woven together into a larger piece. Although it is short, it may actually be difficult to write because of this very compression.

Evan Connell's novel *Mrs. Bridge*, for instance, is arranged as a series of vignettes, each of which seems to stand on its own as a moment captured in a life:

The Search for Love

...As time went on, she felt an increasing need for re-assurance. Her husband had never been a demonstrative man, not even when they were first married; consequently, she did not expect too much from him. Yet there were moments when she was overwhelmed by a terrifying, inarticulate need. One evening as she and he were finishing supper together, alone, the children having gone out, she inquired rather sharply if he loved her. She was surprised by her own bluntness and by the almost shrewish tone of her voice, because that was not the way she actually felt. She saw him gazing at her in astonishment; his expression said very clearly: Why on earth do you think I'm here if I don't love you? Why aren't I somewhere else? What in the world has got into you?

Mrs. Bridge smiled across the floral centerpiece—and it occurred to her that these flowers she had so carefully arranged on the table were what separated her from her husband—and said, a little wretchedly, "I know it's silly, but it's been such a long time since you told me.

Mr. Bridge grunted and finished his coffee. She knew it was not that he was annoyed, only that he was incapable of the kind of declaration she needed. It was so little, and yet so much. While they sat across from each other, neither knowing quite what to do next, she became embarrassed; and in her embarrassment she moved her feet and she inadvertently stepped on the buzzer, concealed beneath the carpet, that connected with the kitchen, with the result that Harriet soon

appeared in the doorway to see what it was that Mrs. Bridge desired.
— Evan Connell (b. 1924)

The final sentence of "The Search for Love" also provides a fine example of the distance a single sentence can travel, through layers of meaning.

Eduardo Galeano, in his three-volume *Memory of Fire*, tells the history of the Americas in a series of short, poignant chapters, which reverberate because of their very compression:

> *1908, San Andrés de Sotavent*
> *The Government Decides that Indians Don't Exist*
>
> The governor, General Miguel Marino Torralvo, issues the order for the oil companies operating on the Colombia coast. The Indians do not exist, the governor certifies before a notary and witnesses. Three years ago, Law No. 1905/55, approved in Bogotá by the National Congress, established that Indians did not exist in San Andrés de Sotavento and other Indian communities where oil had suddenly spurted from the ground.
> —Eduardo Galeano (b. 1940)

*   *   *

- Write about an event in history. Imitate Galeano's compression of events. (See also Michael Harper's "American History" in *History, Herstory*.)

- Write a vignette about family life. Start, perhaps, with your favorite anecdote, which you have only shared aloud. Choose one which has a clear opening and closure. Let it find its way to paper. As you write others, you may find that, together, they build a continuous story: of a family, a job, a love.

Letters Sent or Unsent

We can all relate to the concept of the letter never sent, whether or not the pages actually fill a secret drawer. Sometimes writing to a person fulfills a need we might have to express: anger, desire, or frustration—and the words don't even need to reach the person's hand.

A letter in verse is referred to as an *epistle*, from the Greek *epistole*, meaning message or letter. The word also derives from the epistles adopted as books of the New Testament. Many poems actually feel like letters, perhaps because of an intended ear or audience. But some pieces identify themselves as letters to an individual, such as Auden's forty-page "Letter to Lord Byron" or Scottish poet Robert Burn's "Epistle to a Young Friend."

In the epistolary form, sometimes, there is a recipient. Sometimes, the intended audience is more than one—a community perhaps—as in Martin Luther King Jr.'s famous "Letter from Birmingham Jail." Consider the following passage from the letter:

> Perhaps it is easy for those who have never felt the stinging darts of segregation to say, "Wait." But when you have seen vicious mobs lynch your mothers and fathers at will and drown your sisters and brothers at whim; when you have seen hate-filled policemen curse, kick and even kill your black brothers and sisters; when you see the vast majority of your twenty million Negro brothers smothering in an airtight cage of poverty in the midst of an affluent society; when you suddenly find your tongue twisted and your speech stammering as you seek to explain to your six-year-old daughter why she can't go to the public amusement park that has just been advertised on television, and see tears welling up in her eyes when she is told that Funtown is closed to colored children, and see ominous clouds of inferiority beginning to form in her little mental sky, and see her beginning to distort her personality by developing an unconscious bitterness toward white people; when you have to concoct an answer for a five-year-old son who is asking: "Daddy, why do white people treat colored people so mean?";

when you take a cross-country drive and find it necessary to
sleep night after night in the uncomfortable corners of your
automobile because no motel will accept you; when you are
humiliated day in and day out by nagging signs reading "white"
and "colored"; when your first name becomes "nigger," your
middle name becomes "boy" (however old you are) and your
last name becomes "John," and your wife and mother are never
given the respected title "Mrs."; when you are harried by day and
haunted by night by the fact that you are a Negro, living
constantly at tiptoe stance, never quite knowing what to expect
next, and are plagued with inner fears and outer resentments;
when you are forever fighting a degenerating sense of
"nobodiness"—then you will understand why we find it difficult
to wait.
   —Martin Luther King Jr. (1929-1968)

You may have noticed the extraordinarily long sentence (over 300
words) in the above passage. The choice of grammatical
construction contributes to the sense of urgency. (See *The Grammar
of the Situation.*)
   Many writers over time have first formed ideas for works in
letters sent to friends, or often to fellow writers, who might help
solidify an idea. Some collections, such as Rilke's *Letter to a Young
Poet*, contain the correspondence between two individuals.
Collections of letters by one of your favorite writers can make for
exciting reading, as you can often delve quite deeply into the life of
the artist.
   Some stories have even been built around the core of such a
letter-center, whether it be the actual correspondence, or the
discovery of an old box of forgotten letters. A.S. Byatt's novel
Possession evolves out of an academic's discovery of a letter, which
sends him on an adventure into the past and towards his own
destiny. The book contains a series of such letters, each imagined
by Byatt, which slowly unravel the story of two historical figures.

* * *

• Write a letter you do not intend to send (to someone you know, or
      perhaps, to some historical figure, or even to the future, or
      your future self, perhaps). Try it as prose or poetry.

• Inhabit a character in your favorite piece of writing, and write a letter from his/her perspective. (See *In Character* for Virginia Woolf's example.)

- Write a letter from an ancestor's perspective. Or, if you have any actual old correspondence, use it as a source of inspiration, as in Hart Crane's "My Grandmother's Love Letters":

    ...There is even room enough
    For the letters of my mother's mother,
    Elizabeth,
    That have been pressed so long
    Into a corner of the roof...

    And I ask myself:
    Are your fingers long enough to play
    Old keys that are but echoes...
            —Hart Crane (1899-1933)

The Grammar of the Situation

In *The Writing Life*, Annie Dillard tells a story of a university student who asked a well-known writer, "Do you think I could be a writer?" The writer responded by asking, "Do you like sentences?" The student in Dillard's account was surprised and somewhat dismayed by the response. "Sentences? Do I like sentences? I am twenty years old, do I like sentences?"

Dillard's classic story addresses the need to take pleasure in the individual components of the art. Good writing has attention to such elements as rhythm, syntax, diction, smooth or startling arrangements, juxtaposition of images, compression and development of narrative. (See *How You Say a Thing.*)

The grammar of a language can make for exciting study. Unfortunately, we are usually introduced to grammar via dry units devoid of context in grade and high school which often turn us from the discipline at an early age. But even something as seemingly dry as punctuation is obviously vital to the rhythm and meaning of a piece. Some years ago, my mother left a humorous note for my father, making a point about punctuation, and signed it:

> Love your wife?
> Love: your wife
> Love your wife!
> Love,
> your wife

It is important to study the way a writer uses particular techniques of grammar to achieve certain purposes. Tom Wolfe, for instance, in an essay "O Rotten Gotham," breaks many rules of grammar expressly on purpose. He uses a run-on sentence half a page long, for instance, to convey the feel of the subject he discusses: overcrowding. The sentence itself is overcrowded. He uses the present participle to show the never-ending nature of the congestion:

> In everyday life in New York—just the usual, getting to work, working in massively congested areas like 42nd Street between Fifth Avenue and Lexington, especially now that the Pan-Am

Building is set there, working in cubicles such as those in the editorial offices at Time-Life, Inc., which Dr. Hall cites as typical of New York's poor handling of space, working in cubicles with low ceilings and, often, no access to a window, while construction crews all over Manhattan drive everybody up the Masonite wall with air-pressure generators with noises up to the boil-a-brain decibel levels, then rushing to get home, piling into subways and trains, fighting for time and space, the usual day in New York—the whole now-normal thing keeps shooting jolts of adrenaline into the body, breaking down the body's defenses and winding up with the work-a-daddy human animal stroked out at the breakfast table with his head apoplexed like a cauliflower out of his $6.95 semispread Pima-cotton shirt and nosed over into a plate of No-Kloresto egg substitute, signing off with the black thrombosis, cancer, kidney, liver, or stomach failure, and the adrenals ooze to a halt, the size of eggplants in July.
     —Tom Wolfe (b. 1930)

Leslie Marmon Silko, in an essay called "Landscape, History, and the Pueblo Imagination," uses techniques such as the conditional voice to inhabit the world of her ancestors and bring it to life:

I imagine the last afternoon of my distant ancestors as warm and sunny for late September. They might have been traveling slowly, bringing the sheep closer to Laguna in preparation for the approach of colder weather....There might have been comfort in the warmth and the sight of the sheep fattening on good pasture which lulled my ancestors into their fatal inattention. They might have had a rifle, whereas the Apaches had only bows and arrows. But there would have been four or five Apache raiders, and the surprise attack would have cancelled any advantage the rifles gave them.
     —Leslie Marmon Silko (b. 1948)

One of my favorite novels, Marilynne Robinson's *Housekeeping*, frequently returns to the conditional voice to speak about the past. The effect is a kind of dream-like quality, a drifting between past to present.

Looking out at the lake one could believe that the Flood had never ended. If one is lost on the water, any hill is Ararat. And below is always the accumulated past, which vanishes but does not vanish, which perishes and remains. If we imagine that

Noah's wife when she was old found somewhere a remnant of the Deluge, she might have walked into it till her widow's dress floated above her head and the water loosened her plaited hair. And she would have left it to her sons to tell the tedious tale of generations. She was a nameless woman, and so at home among all those who were never found and never missed, who were uncommemorated, whose deaths were not remarked, nor their begettings.

—Marilynne Robinson (b. 1944)

Robinson's choice of language is also a beautiful example of poetry within prose. If you read the above passage aloud, you will notice the rhythm of the sentences, the near iambic lines such as "If one is lost on the water, any hill is Ararat," "If we imagine that Noah's wife when she was old," or "whose deaths were not remarked nor their begettings" (See *The Weave of Meter.*) She even uses internal assonance (such as *past* and *vanish*, or *tale* and *hair)* and alliteration (such as *tedious tale).* There are parallel structures such as "which vanishes but does not vanish, which perishes and remains" and "who were never found and never missed, who were uncommemorated, whose deaths were not remarked." Notice also the variation of sentence length and structure. Much of the music of this type of passage is best heard, however, when read aloud.

* * *

• Return to the rules of grammar with a different approach (get a book on style). Try reading your favorite piece with grammar-discerning eyes. See how the writer uses, bends, or breaks the rules of grammar for any rhythmic or connotative purposes.

• Using Tom Wolfe's above sentence as a model, write a run-on sentence about the hectic quality of a single day, using the present participle to suggest the ongoing nature of responsibilities.

• Using the excerpts from Silko and Robinson as models, try writing about an ancestor or an historical figure using the conditional voice.

(Note the different parts of speech in "Bilingual/Bilingüe" in *Committing a Rhyme.*)

Parallel Lines

Parallel structures are another type of grammatical tool in prose or poetry. The repetitions are often used to reinforce a statement and create a certain rhythm. Great orators such as Martin Luther King Jr. were known for employing this structure, in works such as the famous "I Have a Dream" speech and "Letter from Birmingham Jail." (See *Letters Sent or Unsent.*)

One well-known example of parallelism is the following verse:

> For want of a nail, the shoe was lost,
> For want of a shoe, the horse was lost,
> For want of a horse, the rider was lost,
> For want of a rider, the battle was lost,
> For want of a battle, the kingdom was lost,
> And all for the want of a horseshoe nail.
> — Benjamin Franklin (1706-1790)

Walt Whitman (1819-1892) often uses a parallel structure to create rhythm in his free verse. The following is an excerpt from Walt Whitman's famous elegy mourning the death of Abraham Lincoln. The repetition of the first word is known as *anaphora*. Notice the way the parallel structure builds the rhythm and contributes to the intensity of the traveling coffin in this excerpt from "When Lilacs Last in the Dooryard Bloomed":

> Coffin that passes through lanes and streets,
> Through day and night with the great cloud darkening the land,
> With the pomp of the inloop'd flags with the cities draped in black,
> With the show of the States themselves as of crape-veil'd women standing,
> With processions long and winding and the flambeaus of the night,
> With the countless torches lit, with the silent sea of faces and the unbared heads,
> With the waiting depot, the arriving coffin, and the sombre faces,

> With dirges through the night, with the thousand voices rising
> strong and solemn,
> With all the mournful voices of the dirges pour'd around the
> coffin,
> The dim-lit churches and the shuddering organs—where amid
> these you journey,
> With the tolling bells' perpetual clang,
> Here, coffin that slowly passes,
> I give you my sprig of lilac.

(See also *Open Season* and "Elegy" in *Occasions for Reflection*.)

Parallel structures exist in Native American traditions as well. Joy Harjo (b. 1951) often uses such repetition, as in "She Had Some Horses," a poem filled with contradictions (or paradox—see *How You Say a Thing*):

> She had horses who called themselves "horse."
> She had horses who called themselves "spirit," and kept
> their voices secret and to themselves...
> She had horses who whispered in the dark, who were afraid to
> speak.
> She had horses who screamed out of fear of the silence, who
> carried knives to protect themselves from ghosts.
> She had horses who waited for destruction.
> She had horses who waited for resurrection.

Many writers also use a parallel structure called *chiasmus* (crossing), in which the word order of one phrase is inverted in the next, as in the following lines which open Christian Wiman's (b. 1966) long narrative poem in blank verse, "The Long Home." The effect is one of elegance within simple language:

> We drove all day on roads without a speck
> Of paving, not knowing but knowing not
> to ask when we would stop or where.

A good example of chiasmus in prose is the following sentence from Marilynne Robinson's *Housekeeping*: "Every sorrow suggests a thousand songs, and every song recalls a thousand sorrows."

* * *

- Write a short prose piece using a parallel structure to emphasize your point and give the passage a certain rhythm.

- To practice chiasmus, list several pairs of words which create an interesting meaning or rhythm. Now incorporate each set into a sentence. A caution: chiasmus can add spice to writing, but just a pinch is often enough.

(For examples of parallel structure by children, see *Dear Star, Do You Know the Moon?*)

The Weave of Meter

Rhythmical patterns of poetry are referred to as *meter* (from the Greek meaning measure). Hearing or reciting a poem with meter gives us a physical, as well as an intellectual or emotional pleasure. Theorists have different conjectures about this physical reaction. Some suggest that it has to do with meter's hypnotic power. Others suggest that the accents in much metered verse are faster than our heartbeats, and so excite and speed up our hearts. Frederick Turner, in his essay "The Neural Lyre," speaks about the effect of metered verse on the brain—that it encourages the left brain to communicate with the right brain. He suggests that our left-brain activity of understanding language becomes infused with our more hard-wired, right brain pattern-recognition abilities, that meter, essentially, tunes up the brain, combining a rhythmic organization with a variety of syntactical possibilities. He speaks of the brain as a *"Penelope*, whose right hand weaves the shroud of meaning and whose left hand disentangles the thread or clue of understanding." He traces how societies have evolved using meter, a cultural universal, perhaps because of its hypnotic power to cast a spell in the mind—a rhythmic reality rooted in science. Dana Gioia, in *Can Poetry Matter*, draws on this recognition of meter as an ancient technique used when there was very "little, if any distinction among poetry, religion, history, music, and magic." All were performed using an incantatory meter.

Poetry written with meter is sometimes called verse, from the Latin *versus*, meaning turned around or back. The structural unit of the line in most poetry (metered or un-metered) has this element of the "turn." The word *line* derives from the Latin *linea*, associated with linen, or thread. One might think of poetry as lines spun together on a loom. The rhythms of language have meaning and are a powerful element of the weave.

It is a good idea to become familiar with the various meters (both the patterns of regularity as well as different methods of variation) and to try your hand at them. It will help you recognize why certain lines have always remained with you and give you additional tools for writing. You may even begin to notice meter in prose passages or in everyday speech. Many lines of everyday speech in English, for instance, tend to the iambic, a pattern of unstressed, stressed syllables. The following are examples of iambic, trochaic, anapestic, and dactylic meter, some methods of variation, and occasional reasons for the writer's particular choice of a certain meter.

iambic: a line consisting primarily of iambs, an unstressed syllable followed by a stressed syllable, as in the following similar laments:

> ⏑ / ⏑ / ⏑ / ⏑ ⏑ ⏑ /
> I **all** | a**lone** | be**weep** | my **out** | cast **state**,
> —William Shakespeare (1564-1616)

> ⏑ / ⏑ / ⏑ / ⏑ / ⏑ /
> Woke **up** | this **mor** | nin', **blues** | all **round** | my **bed**.
> — traditional

trochaic: line consisting mainly of *trochees*, a stressed syllable followed by an unstressed syllable. Trochaic meter is often used to convey a kind of mystical quality, such as Blake's "Tyger, Tyger" (See *Dear Star, Do You Know the Moon)* or the following:

> / ⏑ / ⏑ / ⏑ / ⏑ / ⏑ / ⏑
> **Once** up|**on** a| **mid**night |**drear**y, **while** I |**pon**dered,|**weak** and
> / ⏑
> **wear**y,
> Over many a quaint and curious volume of forgotten lore—
> While I nodded, nearly napping, suddenly there came a tapping,
> As of someone gently rapping, rapping at my chamber door.
> "Tis some visitor," I muttered, "tapping at my chamber door—
> Only this and nothing more."
> —Edgar Allan Poe (1809-1849)

(See "Spells and Trochaic Meter" in *Spells, Prophecies and Prayers*.)

anapestic: line consisting mainly of *anapests*, two unstressed syllables followed by a stressed syllable. Note the galloping pace of these lines from Robert Browning's poem, "How We Brought the Good News from Ghent to Aix," created by the use of the anapest:

> ⏑ ⏑ / ⏑ ⏑ / ⏑ ⏑ / ⏑ ⏑ /
> And his **low** | head and **crest**, |just one **sharp** |ear bent **back**
> For my voice, and the other pricked out on his track;
> And one eye's black intelligence,—ever that glance
> O'er its white edge at me, his own master, askance!
> —Robert Browning (1812-1889)

In "Confederacy," the anapests feel like a dance, like Paschen's "two-stepping" subject:

> Wear the **heart** | like a **home**
> as in Patsy Kline's song,
> what we're two-stepping to...
> —Elise Paschen

dactylic: line consisting mainly of *dactyls* (one stressed syllable followed by two unstressed syllables.

> **This** is the | **for**est pri | **me**val. The | **mur**muring   **pines**
> and the | **hem**lock
> —Henry Wadsworth Longfellow (1807-1882)

June Jordan chose to use dactyls in her poem for Phyllis Wheatley (the poet slave who, in the eighteenth century, was the first woman, as well as the first African American to publish a book in North America). Jordan's choice of form for this poem echoes Wheatley's poetry:

> ...**Viewed** like a | **spe**cies of | **flaw** in the | **live**stock
> A child without safety of mother or marriage.
> Chosen by whimsy but born to surprise
> They taught you to read but you learned how to write...
> —June Jordan (b. 1936)

Variations in regularity—or metrical substitutions—are a vital aspect of meter. There are many ways one can create variation. In iambic meter, for instance, trochaic feet often appear at the beginning of lines for emphasis. In "Welcome to Hiroshima," trochaic feet such as "Jammed on" break the iambic meter for emphasis.

> ...the wristwatch of a child.
> **Jammed** on | the **mo**|ment's **im**|pact, **re** | so**lute**
> —Mary Jo Salter (b. 1954)

The *pyrrhic* foot is another common substitution, consisting of two unstressed syllables:

∪ / ∪ / ∪ / ∪ ∪ ∪ /
A **horse**! | A **Horse**! | My **king** | dom for | a **horse**!
—William Shakespeare (1564-1616)

And the *spondee* contains two stressed syllables:

∪ / ∪ / ∪ / ∪ / / /
Yet **once** | more **ere** | thou **hate** | me, **one** | **full kiss**.
—A.C. Swinburne (1837-1909)

In "Single Sonnet," Bogan struggles with the "heroic mould" of the sonnet, which "proves" its strength and returns to iambic in her final line:

/ / ∪ / / ∪∪ / ∪ /
Staunch meter, |**great song**, |it is **yours**, |at **length,**
To prove how stronger you are than my strength.
—Louise Bogan (1897-1970)

Two other ways to add variety to a line are use of the *caesura*, or pause, usually indicated by punctuation and use of *enjambment*, or a line which runs on to the next without a pause (as opposed to an *end-stopped* line). The following two lines illustrate both devices:

Lose something every day. Accept the fluster
of lost door keys, the hour badly spent.
—Elizabeth Bishop (1911-1979)

Samuel Taylor Coleridge wrote the following lines to help memorize the different meters. Each line depicts the meter it describes:

Trochee trips from long to short;
From long to long in solemn sort
Slow Spondee stalks, strong foot, yet ill able
Ever to come up with Dactyl trisyllable.
Iambics march from short to long;
With a leap and a bound the swift Anapests throng.
—Samuel Taylor Coleridge (1772-1834)

Iambic and anapestic meters are called *rising* meters, as they move from unstressed to stressed syllables. Trochaic and dactylic meters are called *falling*. One might think of the meter of lines as landscape, with hills and valleys of different size or levels of stress.

Meter creates the pattern, which then allows certain variations to have more impact. The amount of variation in a poem can range from very little to extensive changes, often depending on the subject.

The unit of a line whose repetition creates the rhythm is called a *foot*. The length of a line is essential to the rhythm of metered poetry as well as open form. In open form, in particular, a line might break at a certain, perhaps unexpected, point for the purpose of creating a particular rhythm or meaning—see *Open Season*. Pentameter, the most common meter, contains five feet. Monometer, dimeter, trimeter, tetrameter, hexameter, heptameter, and octameter contain one, two, three, four, six, seven, and eight beats, respectively:

monometer: one beat, a rare line length, as in the following epigram:

> Adam
> Had 'em.
> —Anonymous

(See *Epigram*.)

dimeter: two beats:

> you've swept
> the shelves
> of spoons
> and plates
> you kept
> for guests
> — Kay Ryan (b. 1945)

trimeter: three beats:

> Up from the bronze, I saw
> Water without a flaw
> Rush to its rest in air,
> Reach to its rest, and fall.
> —Louise Bogan (1897-1970)

tetrameter: four beats:

> Whose woods these are, I think I know.
> His house is in the village, though.
> He will not see me stopping here
> to watch his woods fill up with snow.
> —Robert Frost (1874-1963)

pentameter: five beats, the most common line in English. This brief example is from Milton's *Paradise Lost* (IX 115-123). Notice, however, that the fourth and ninth lines of the excerpt break the meter and have six beats. The list of "rocks, dens, and caves" recalls an earlier description in book two of the epic: "Rocks, caves, lakes, fens, bogs, dens, and shades of death" (see *octameter*, below):

> If I could joy in aught; sweet interchange
> of hill and valley, rivers, woods, and plains,
> Now land, now sea and shores with forest crowned,
> Rocks, dens, and caves! But I in none of these
> find place or refuge; and the more I see
> Pleasures about me, so much more I feel
> Torment within me, as from the hateful siege
> Of contraries; all good to me becomes
> Bane, and in Heaven much worse would be my state.
> —John Milton (1608-1674)

hexameter: six beats, sometimes called an *alexandrine*:

> I will arise and go now, and go to Innisfree,
> And a small cabin build there, of clay and wattles made.
> Nine bean-rows will I have there, a hive for the honey-bee,
> And live alone in the bee-loud glade.
> — William Butler Yeats (1865-1939)

heptameter: seven beats these are often called *fourteeners*. They were common in the Renaissance, but are rather uncommon now. "Casey at the Bat" is a famous American poem in heptameter:

> The outlook wasn't brilliant for the mudville nine that day;
> The score stood four to two with but one inning more to play.
> —Ernest Lawrence Thayer (1863-1940)

Some metrists suggest that ballad meter is a derivation of heptameter, with its pattern of four stresses, then three, as in the following excerpt from "The Rime of the Ancient Mariner":

> Since then, at an uncertain hour,
> That agony returns
> And till my ghastly tale is told,
> This heart within me burns.
> — Samuel Taylor Coleridge (1772-1834)

octameter: eight beats, a very uncommon line in English. Swinburne's "March" is one example. Some octameter lines exist as dramatic variations from other patterns to make meaning, such as:

Rocks, caves, lakes, fens, bogs, dens, and shades of death.
— John Milton (1608-1674)

Lines longer than eight beats exist, but they are quite rare, probably because of the limitations imposed by the natural rhythm of breathing.

Some poets, most notably Marianne Moore, have enjoyed working in *syllabics* (arranging lines by syllables, but without attention to meter). Syllabic verse is sometimes confused with *accentual* verse. Accentual verse refers to amount and pattern of stresses, not merely the number of syllables. Ballad meter, for instance, contains a wide variety of syllable counts per line, but a precise pattern of stresses or accents. (See *Ballads and Bal-lades*.) Richard Wilbur's "Junk" is a good example of a contemporary use of accentual meter, with four beats in each line. (See excerpt in *Ars Poetica*.)

Accentual-syllabic verse is the term for meter which keeps a precise pattern of syllables and accents, with variation occurring in the accents. Accentual syllabic meter is the basis for standard English meters such as iambic pentameter.

Sprung rhythm, introduced by Gerard Manley Hopkins, is a blending of accentual meter with the feet of accentual-syllabic meter. Hopkins disliked the "common measure" of other Victorians and chose to develop a stronger, more vital verse. In his system, each foot begins with a stress and might consist of any number of syllables, even a single stressed syllable. The line is measured by the number of stresses, which fall within normal word stress (and are not necessarily separated by unstressed syllables).

Quantitative meter, common among the classical forms of the ancient Greeks and Romans, is based on the principle of vowel length (the time it takes to say a syllable).

Metrically, the English interpretation of *Sapphics* work better than other translations of classical forms. Sapphics (named for the Greek poet Sappho), but also used by Catullus and Horace, are four-line stanzas in the meter of the example below. The term "sapphics" is also used to refer to the meter of the first three lines of each stanza. The English Sapphic stanza consists of three eleven-syllable lines—hendecasyllables, followed by a five-syllable line, with the stresses noted below:

ANNIE FINCH (b. 1956)

Sapphics for Patience

Look there—**some**thing **rests** on your **hand** and **e**ven
lingers, though the wind all around is asking
it to leave you. Passing the open passage,
you have been **cho**sen.

Seed. Like dust or thistle it sits so lightly
that your hand while holding the trust of silk gets
gentle. Seed like hope has come, making stillness.
Wish in the quiet.

If I stood there—stopped by an open passage—
staring at my hand—which is always open—
hopeful, maybe, not to compel you, I'd wish
only for patience.

The fifth and eleventh syllables of the long lines may be either stressed or unstressed. The last syllable of the short line can be either stressed or unstressed.

A difficulty of the Sapphic stanza may be its inflexible meter (due to an attempt to imitate classical syllable quantities), which may not allow for shifts in rhythm to create meaning. Some poets have used the basic structure of the Sapphic stanza, with small metrical variations, or with a looser pattern of five beats per line, for instance.

When using meter, our minds and bodies respond to both the regularity and the change. As Robert Bridges said, "the rhythm beneath allows the poem to lift off." Practicing different meters is also likely to give your free verse and your prose a more lyrical quality, as you train your ear.

(For a far more extensive discussion of the many intricacies of meter, a comprehensive source is Timothy Steele's book on meter, *All the Fun's in How You Say a Thing*.)

* * *

152

- Try writing lines with the different basic meters (iambic, trochaic, etc.). You might listen to everyday speech and write down lines that have a particular rhythm.

- Find a passage of prose in which a few sentences follow basic metrical patterns: Break them into lines and then *feet* (the metrical subdivisions of a line) and note their *scansion* (the process of applying symbols of stress). You could use Marilynne Robinson's excerpt in *The Grammar of the Situation* for this exercise.

- Note how such elements as caesura and enjambment affect rhythm. Try writing lines with these elements. (See also *Committing a Rhyme*.)

- Write a poem in iambic pentameter. Find one or more places in the poem where a break in the meter might be used to create a particular meaning (as in the examples of variation noted). Practice techniques of variation (trochees, pyrrhic, spondaic feet).

- Practice writing lines that have accentual rhythm. Create a pattern of a certain number of beats per line (tetrameter, pentameter, etc.).

- Read your own writing aloud (poetry and prose). It will help you hear the undercurrents of your own rhythm (or identify where it needs work).

Committing a Rhyme

Early on in workshops, my students often ask me if they are "allowed to rhyme" in a poem. Much of the modern work they come across has no meter or rhyme. Earlier in the twentieth century, I imagine students asked for permission *not* to rhyme. Most of the models of rhyme which an average anthology contains are poems from other centuries, so when students try to use certain patterns of sound, they often write using archaic language and syntax. Many people have not come in contact with good contemporary models of poems using rhyme (other than songs, which are often considered another category). We learn by example, and it is important to learn from the great poets of our history, but also to have contemporary models. (The other chapters in this section offer many good models of contemporary use of rhyme.)

In Bruce Meyer's interview with British poet James Fenton in the late 1980's, Fenton suggests that there are many poets writing today who are terrified of "committing a rhyme." He states that one must defy the unspoken and spoken rules of the critics and the fads:

> Absolutely defy it. If you don't defy it, you're going to be a prisoner of your time... When I was teaching in Minnesota, I learned a lot about how people can be cowed into submission by critical opinion. The terror with which they treated the question of form, as if there is a question of form. There isn't a question of form. There is poetry. There is this terrific art which has been handed down from generation to generation to read with immense pleasure. But there are some people who are sitting there terrified of committing a rhyme...

Rhyme requires practice and a good ear, or it can fail miserably. A bad poem in rhyme is more loud (cacophonous, perhaps) and noticeable than a bad free verse poem, which might just quietly die on the page. English is a difficult language in which to use rhyme, for it contains far fewer rhyming words when compared with Spanish or Italian, for instance. Variations broaden the musical possibilities in English and often allow for lines which sound more natural to the ear. There are many ways to create variation, either by using the following different types of rhyme, or by alternating the parts of speech at the end of lines, or by such techniques as *enjambment* (discussed in an exercise below). Writers often use these techniques without realizing what has created the music. After awhile, these methods become second nature.

Rhyme and its variations must have meaning, just as rhythm does. A deliberate *off rhyme* (discussed below) among exact rhymes, for instance, might create the deliberate effect of disorder or letdown. Emily Dickinson was particularly fond of slant rhyme and used it a great deal. The off rhyme has a powerful effect in the following short poem, where the rhyme feels "dropt" along with the cutlery:

EMILY DICKINSON (1830-1886)

The Lightning is a Yellow Fork

The Lightning is a yellow Fork
From Tables in the sky
By inadvertent fingers dropt
The awful Cutlery

Of mansions never quite disclosed
And never quite concealed
The Apparatus of the Dark
To ignorance revealed.

The following are patterns of sound and types of rhyme (defined as the repetition of the identical or similar stressed sound):

exact rhyme: Differing consonant sounds, followed by identical stressed vowel sounds: state—gate, lies—surprise (there are numerous examples in the following chapters).

off rhyme (also called slant-rhyme, half rhyme, near rhyme, approximate rhyme, oblique rhyme): The sounds are similar, but not exactly alike. In the most common type of slant rhyme, the final consonant sounds are identical, but the stressed vowel sounds differ. This effect might exist at the end or in the middle of a line, and is referred to as consonance: good—food, soot—flute. (See "Pantoum for Chinese Women" in *Pantoum*.)

assonance: The repetition, in proximity, of identical vowel sounds, preceded and followed by differing consonant sounds: ten—them, time—mine. (See *"Memento Mori* in Middle School" in *Old Myth, New Myth.*)

alliteration: The repetition of initial consonant sounds: bubbles breaking/bread/bore, or sometimes the prominent repetition of the first consonant: *after life's final.*

masculine rhyme (single rhyme): The final syllables are stressed, and after their initial consonant sounds, are identical in sound: spent—meant—intent. (See "One Art" in *Villanelle*, among many examples.)

feminine rhyme (also known as double rhyme): Stressed rhymed syllables are followed by identical unstressed syllables: master—disaster—fluster, despising—arising. (See "One Art" in *Villanelle* and "When in Disgrace with Fortune and Men's Eyes" in *Sonnet.*)

triple rhyme: A form of feminine rhyme, in which identical stressed vowel sounds are followed by two identical unstressed syllables: goddesses—bodices—Odysseys, apology—mythology. This type of rhyme works well occasionally, but has the greatest likelihood of slipping into light verse. It might be best employed in deliberately humorous verse. (See excerpt from Byron's *Don Juan* in *Stanzas.*)

eye rhyme: The sounds do not rhyme, but the words look as if they would rhyme: rough—bough.

end rhyme (also known as terminal rhyme): Rhymes which appear at the end of lines.

internal rhyme: Rhymes which appear within the line: Stack to Stack/and the built hayrack back. The rhymes in quick succession create the effect of the horses' machine-like tasks. (See "Names of Horses" in *Occasions for Reflection.*)

Two important cautions, to avoid the most common failures of rhyme in contemporary verse: Don't go for the easiest rhyme. Rhyme should surprise. Secondly, don't use awkward syntax just to squeeze in a rhyme. It didn't work for Cinderella's stepsisters. Or, to reference another tale, if you force a rhyme, it will beat like a tell-tale heart in the center of your poem.

*   *   *

- Write lines practicing each of the above elements of rhyme (exact rhyme, off rhyme, etc.).

- Running one line into the next, or *enjambment* (also discussed in *The Weave of Meter*), rather than using end-stopped lines, can enhance the flow and keep rhymes from sounding too lockstep. Notice the enjambment in Rhina Espaillat's poem, "Bilingual/Bilingüe" below. Practice using enjambment to soften the sound of exact rhymes.

- Another way to keep rhyme fresh and interesting (exact rhyme, in particular), is to vary your choice of parts of speech for the rhyming word. Write some lines which vary the parts of speech. End your lines with a verb, then a noun, then an adjective, etc., as in the example below:

RHINA P. ESPAILLAT (b. 1932)

Bilingual/Bilingüe

My father liked them separate, one there,	(adverb)
one here (allá y aqui), as if aware	(adjective)
that words might cut in two his daughter's heart	(noun)
(el corazón) and lock the alien part	(noun)
to what he was—his memory, his name	(noun)
(su nombre)—with a key he could not claim.	(verb)

English outside this door, Spanish inside," (preposition)
he said, "y basta." But who can divide (verb)

the world, the word (mundo y palabra) from (preposition)
any child? I knew how to be dumb (adjective)

and stubborn (testaruda); late, in bed, (noun)
I hoarded secret syllables I read (verb)

Until my tongue (mi lengua) learned to run (verb)
where his stumbled. And still the heart was one. (noun)

I like to think he knew that, even when, (conjunction)
proud (orgulloso) of his daughter's pen, (noun)

he stood outside mis versos, half in fear (noun)
of words he loved but wanted not to hear. (verb)

(See also *The Grammar of the Situation* and Robert Frost's "The Road Not Taken" in *How You Say a Thing*.)

Stanzas

Many poems are organized in stanzas, or groups of lines. *Stanza* comes from the Italian, meaning room, or stopping place. The following is a very brief overview of stanza forms with a few examples, as well as a few suggestions of other poems to seek out on your own. The overview is intended to give you a sense of the way you might break your own poems into traditional stanza forms, or use such structures as points of departure. Poems broken into stanzas need not necessarily rhyme, of course, but the following examples offer both classical and contemporary examples of rhyme, as well.

Many poems are arranged in couplets (units of two lines), from the heroic verse of Dryden and Pope to such familiar poems as Blake's "The Tyger." Often couplets are only distinguished by the rhyme scheme (aabbcc, etc.). Some couplets are arranged in a structure of two-line stanzas, as in Cunningham's "In the Thirtieth Year:"

> In the thirtieth year of life
> I took my heart to be my wife,
>
> And as I turn in bed by night
> I have my heart for my delight...
> —J.V. Cunningham (1911-1985)

(See *Ghazal* and "Bilingual/Bilingüe" in *Committing a Rhyme.*)

Three-line stanzas, or **tercets**, might carry different rhyme schemes. Marilyn Nelson's "Chosen" is an example of tercets (with a varying rhyme scheme) which form a sonnet. (See "Chosen" in *Sonnet.*)

All three lines of the tercet might also rhyme, for instance:

> The Angel that presided o'er my birth
> Said little creature formed of joy and mirth
> Go love without the help of anything on earth.
> —William Blake (1757-1827)

The following example breaks the rhythm and alters the rhyme for the purpose of slowing the poem down at its closure:

> Stillness after motion,
> the creaky music cranking, cranking down,
> the carnival preparing to leave town.
> —Rachel Hadas (b. 1948)

Another common rhyme scheme for a three-line stanza is *terza rima* (triple rhyme) such as Dante used. The rhyme scheme is aba, bcb, cdc, etc. The middle rhyme of each tercet becomes the first and third rhyme of the next stanza. The interlocking form weaves the stanzas together and gives the poem movement, propelling it forward. Frost's "Acquainted With the Night" uses this rhyme, although, interestingly, the poem might also be considered a sonnet. (For a variation on terza rima, see "*Memento Mori* in Middle School" in *Old Myth, New Myth*.)

The quatrain or four-line stanza is the most common in European literature. The quatrain used most often is the ballad stanza, with four beats in the first and third lines, three in the second and fourth. Emily Dickinson used this form in most of her poems:

EMILY DICKINSON (1830-1886)

Tell all the Truth But Tell it Slant

Tell all the Truth but tell it slant—
Success in Circuit lies
Too bright for our infirm Delight
The Truth's superb surprise

As Lightning to the Children eased
With explanation kind
The Truth must dazzle gradually
Or every man be blind—

(See *Ballad and Ballade* and *Pantoum*.)

The five-line stanza allows for many combinations of rhymes and line lengths. Edgar Allen Poe uses the familiar quatrain and adds an additional rhyming line:

EDGAR ALLEN POE (1809-1849)

To Helen

Helen, thy beauty is to me
    Like those Nicéan barks of yore,
That gently, o'er a perfumed sea,
    The weary, way-worn wanderer bore
To his own native shore.

On desperate seas long wont to roam,
    Thy hyacinth hair, thy classic face,
Thy Naiad airs have brought me home
    To the glory that was Greece,
And the grandeur that was Rome.

Lo! in yon brilliant window-niche
    How statue-like I see thee stand,
    The agate lamp within thy hand!
Ah, Psyche, from the regions which
    Are Holy-Land!

(See Robert Frost's "The Road Not Taken" in *How You Say a Thing.*)

The six-line stanza might contain one of many different patterns of rhyme and meter. The "Venus and Adonis" stanza, named for Shakespeare's poem, is a quatrain with a couplet, rhyming ababcc. The "Burns stanza" or "Scottish stanza" follows a pattern of aaabab—the a's tetrameter (four feet), the b's dimeter (two feet). R.S. Gwynn's "The Classroom at the Mall" uses abccab:

> Our Dean of Something thought it would be good
> For Learning (even better for P.R.)
> To make the school 'accessible to all'
> And leased the bankrupt bookstore at the Mall
> A few steps from Poquito's Mexican Food
> And Chocolate Chips Aweigh. So here we are —
>   —R.S. Gwynn (b. 1948)

(See *Sestina.*)

The seven-line stanza also offers many possibilities. *Rime royal* (so named because it was used by King James I) is the most common. It contains iambic pentameter, rhyming ababbcc. But many contemporary poets have created their own seven-line structures:

> My frowning students carve
> Me monsters out of prose:
> This one—a gargoyle—thumbs its contemptuous nose
> At how, in English, subject must agree
> With verb—for any such agreement shows
> Too great a willingness to serve,
> A docility
> —Charles Martin (b. 1942)

Ottava rima is the most widely known eight-line stanza: iambic pentameter abababcc—familiar to many through Yeats' "Among School Children," or in Byron's witty *Don Juan*:

> His classic studies made a little puzzle,
> Because of filthy loves of gods and goddesses,
> Who in the earlier ages raised a bustle,
> But never put on pantaloons or bodices;
> His reverend tutors had at times a tussle,
> And for their Aeneiads, Iliads and Odysseys,
> Were forced to make an odd sort of apology,
> For Donna Inez dreaded the Mythology.
> —George Gordon, Lord Byron (1788-1824)

Fred D'Aguiar's *Bloodlines* is a contemporary narrative in ottava rima:

> And now I have to make a confession.
> I said way back that I can't die, sure,
> but the real truth is I won't die, not as long
> as slavery harnesses history, driving her
> over the edge, into the ground, to exhaustion.
> I refuse to lie in ground whose pressure,
> shaped like my body, is not six feet of soil,
> but slavery; not history on me, but forced toil.
> —Fred D'Aguiar (b. 1960)

The *Spenserian stanza* (as used in *The Faeire Queen*) is the classic nine-line form. The first eight lines have iambic pentameter and the ninth is an alexandrine (with twelve syllables). The rhyme scheme is ababbcbcc. Byron, Shelley and other Romantics enjoyed the elaborate musical quality of the interlacing form. The following is the first stanza of Shelley's famous elegy for John Keats, "Adonais:"

> I weep for Adonais—he is dead!
> Oh, weep for Adonais! though our tears
> Thaw not the frost which binds so dear a head!
> And thou sad Hour, selected from all years
> To mourn our loss, rouse thy obscure compeers,
> And teach them thine own sorrow, say: with me
> Died Adonais; till the Future dares
> Forget the Past, his fate and fame shall be
> An echo and a light unto eternity!
> —Percy Bysshe Shelley (1792-1822)

(See the chapter *Occasions for Reflection* for elegies.)

Timothy Steele's "The Library" is a good contemporary example of the nine-line stanza:

> I could construct a weighty paradigm,
> The Library as Mind. It's somehow truer
> To recollect details of closing time.
> Someone, at slotted folders on a viewer,
> Tucks microfiche squares in their resting places;
> Felt cloth's drawn over the exhibit cases;
> The jumbled New Book Shelves are set in shape;
> The days' last check-outs are thumped quickly through a
> Device that neutralizes tattle-tape.
> —Timothy Steele (b. 1948)

Some forms have no fixed stanzas, but continue until they end. *Blank verse* (unrhymed iambic pentameter) is the best known pattern for poems in English. Most parts of Shakespeare's plays are in blank verse, as is Milton's *Paradise Lost*. Many twentieth century writers such as Robert Frost and Elizabeth Bishop have found blank verse to be an ideal form for conveying the natural rhythms of language. Numerous contemporary writers such as Dana Gioia, Emily Grosholz, Mark Jarman, Dave Mason, Robert McDowell, Mary

Jo Salter, and Christian Wiman (to name just a few) continue in this tradition, often using the form to sustain longer narrative poems, sometimes book-length works.

ROBERT FROST (1874-1963)

The Mending Wall

Something there is that doesn't love a wall,
That sends the frozen-ground-swell under it,
And spills the upper boulders in the sun;
And makes gaps even two can pass abreast.
The work of hunters is another thing:
I have come after them and made repair
Where they have left not one stone on a stone,
But they would have the rabbit out of hiding,
To please the yelping dogs. The gaps I mean,
No one has seen them made or heard them made,
But at spring mending-time we find them there.
I let my neighbor know beyond the hill;
And on a day we meet to walk the line
And set the wall between us once again.
We keep the wall between us as we go.
To each the boulders that have fallen to each.
And some are loaves and some so nearly balls
We have to use a spell to make them balance:
"Stay where you are until our backs are turned!"
We wear our fingers rough with handling them.
Oh, just another kind of outdoor game,
One on a side. It comes to little more:
There where it is we do not need the wall:
He is all pine and I am apple orchard.
My apple trees will never get across
And eat the cones under his pines, I tell him.
He only says, 'Good fences make good neighbors.'
Spring is the mischief in me, and I wonder
If I could put a notion in his head:
'Why do they make good neighbors? Isn't it
Where there are cows? But here there are no cows.
Before I built a wall I'd ask to know
What I was walling in or walling out
And to whom I was like to give offense.
Something there is that doesn't love a wall,

That wants it down.' I could say 'Elves' to him,
But it's not elves exactly, and I'd rather
He said it for himself. I see him there
Bringing a stone grasped firmly by the top
In each hand, like an old-stone savage armed.
He moves in darkness as it seems to me,
Not of woods and the shade of trees.
He will not go behind his father's saying,
And he likes having thought of it so well
He says again, 'Good fences make good neighbors.'

*   *   *

- Try your hand at the different stanza forms. Pay attention to certain shapes and structures which may emerge in your journal. Notice, for instance, if a poem seems to be developing in couplets. Model your favorite poets. You will probably find that certain divisions suit your particular voice or certain subjects better than others.

Open Season (Open Form Poetry)

Free verse is the translation of *vers libre*, which arose in France in the late nineteenth century, partially in response to strict structural rules of the past regarding such things as precise placement of caesura (or pause) in the line, and counting of syllables. Vers libre began as a relaxation of these rules. The early twentieth century in America brought free verse to the forefront, the new philosophies encapsulated in Ezra Pound's famous statement that one should "compose in the sequence of the musical phrase, not the metronome."

The name free verse, however, has often been debated and called inaccurate and misleading because it implies that there are no limitations or guiding principles. Other terms are sometimes preferred, "open form poetry," for instance.

Ironically, memorable poetry in open form can be very difficult to write because of the discipline which such freedom demands. The unit of free verse is often described as being a breath. The form requires an attention to the cadences of language. Each phrase should be weighed carefully, as should the length of a line. Rhythm is a vital aspect of open form. One of the dangers of "free verse" is that it sometimes implies to beginners that "anything goes." Much poetry being written today exists on the page, but not in the ear. Arbitrary line breaks and a lack of rhythm can be the unfortunate result.

As any teacher knows, students sometimes want to declare "open season" on all rules (grammatical, formal, etc.). Certain "seasons" in one's writing can be useful (as many exercises in this book suggest). It is important to remember, however (though I don't love extending the hunting metaphor), that the point of open season is not to obliterate all of the animals in the forest.

When discussing the origins of free verse, it is vital to remember that the poets who introduced it into contemporary society had been trained in traditional forms. Poets such as Whitman, Pound, Eliot, and Stevens have undercurrents of form in their free verse. But even earlier "formal" poets such as John Milton, William Blake, and Matthew Arnold used radical departures from meter or rhyme schemes before such action had a name and popularity.

There are different conjectures as to the reasons for the development of free verse in America. American writers may have been endeavoring to cast off English forms. Walt Whitman, one of the best known American writers of free verse, has great musicality and rhythm in his lines which reflect the landscapes of his American heritage. His lines have a rising or a falling quality based on the rhythm. One frequently hears pairs of lines with the same meter. Whitman often creates rhythms using parallel structures. (See *Parallel Lines.*) In the following poem, notice the way the rhythm builds with the increasing number of beats in the first few lines:

WALT WHITMAN (1819-1892)

When I Heard the Learned Astronomer

When I heard the learn'd astronomer,
When the proofs, the figures, were ranged in columns before
    me,
When I was shown the charts and diagrams, to add, divide, and
    measure them,
When I sitting heard the astronomer where he lectured with
    much applause in the lecture-room,
How soon unaccountable I became tired and sick,
till rising and gliding out I wander'd off by myself,
In the mystical moist night-air, and from time to time,
Look'd up in perfect silence at the stars.

Whitman also employs other techniques of repetition to make rhythm, such as the grammatical use of the present participle to achieve a "continual" effect in the following lines from "Song of Myself":

Many sweating, ploughing, thrashing, and then the chaff for
    payment receiving.
A few idly owning, and they the wheat continually claiming.

(See also *The Grammar of the Situation.*)

Poems in open form sometimes follow a basic metrical pattern and might occasionally be characterized in metrical terms: a poem might be said to have a loose *dactylic* rhythm, for instance. (See *The Weave of Meter.*) Some poetry has no verse lines and is referred to as *prose poetry*, as in this excerpt from "The Colonel":

> ...The colonel returned with a sack used to bring groceries home. He spilled many human ears on the table. They were like dried peach halves. There is no other way to say this. He took one of them in his hands, shook it in our faces, dropped it in a water glass. It came alive there...He swept the ears to the floor with his arm and held the last of his wine in the air. Something for your poetry, no? he said...
> —Carolyn Forche (b. 1950)

Genre distinctions are often blurred. A vignette, for instance, might sometimes be considered a prose poem. (See *Vignette.*)

Poetry often has an attention to the shape on the page, which translates to the ear. *Visual* or *concrete* poetry is the term for the particular kind of poetry in which the words form actual shapes: a bird, wings, a flower, etc. But open form poetry can take on interesting shapes based on subject and should have good reason for its line breaks. May Swenson's "The Shape of Death" is an example of a poem whose form on the page was altered to create a distinct rhythm and meaning. Swenson wrote the poem ten years after the bombing of Hiroshima and Nagasaki. Originally, the poem was structured:

> there is a clap of sound, a white blossom
> belches from the jaw of fright,
> a pillared cloud churns from white to gray
> like a monstrous brain that bursts and burns,
> then turns sickly black, spilling away,
> filling the whole sky with ashes of dread...
> —May Swenson (1913-1989)

In a later version, Swenson rearranged her poem, "re-membering" them by dismembering them, creating the effect of what is blown apart:

	There is a
clap of sound. A white	blossom belches from the
jaw of fright. A	monstrous brain that bursts
and burns—then turns	sickly black, spilling
away, filling the whole	sky with ashes of dread.

Good open form poetry has rhythm, whether it be a fluidity or an intentionally jarring pattern of sound to create a certain effect. One element is essential in all writing: poets need to train and use their ears.

* * *

• Read aloud some free verse poems whose lines have remained with you. Identify any metrical patterns within. (See *The Weave of Meter.*) What kind of patterns exist? Is there a reason for the line breaks?

• Experiment with line breaks. Consider Swenson's deliberate jarring effect in the above excerpt. Choose a subject which would benefit from such a chaotic structure and rhythm and use the line breaks to create meaning.

• Take a familiar passage of prose which you find rhythmical, and break it into lines. Pay attention to the rhythm of the prose and to your reasons for breaking each line. Use such elements as caesura (or pauses) in a line to help create the rhythm. In a workshop, you might each do the same passage of prose, and discuss the similarities and differences which result.

• In all writing (but in free verse, in particular) the rhythm often relies on word choice or particular combinations of sound, such as internal rhyme or alliteration. (See *Committing a Rhyme.*) Combinations of words can create a fluid pace or a harsh breaking rhythm. Sometimes such rhythms appear beneath your pen. Harvest your freewriting to find some of these combinations. Build on the structures you find.

Epigram

The epigram is a short, often witty poem, meant to be remembered. The word derives from the Greek word meaning "write on," on a gravestone or a wall, for instance. Such writing tended to be brief, given the limited space, not to mention the labor of carving each letter in stone. *The Greek Anthology* is an ancient collection of over 1500 epigrams of all kinds. Epigrams have survived from antiquity in many languages (probably because they were carved in stone) and convey such subjects as history, irony, and love. The following is a translation of an early Persian poet:

> I'll hide within my poems as I write them
> Hoping to kiss your lips as you recite them.
> —Amareh (11th century)
> trans. Dick Davis

An epigram need not rhyme or follow a particular meter, although very many do, given the nature of the form as one to be remembered. Rhyme certainly enhances that intention.

> Sir, I admit your general rule,
> That every poet is a fool:
> But you yourself may serve to show it,
> That every fool is not a poet.
> — Alexander Pope (1688-1744)

> John, while swimming in the ocean,
> rubbed sharks' backs with suntan lotion.
> Now the sharks have skin of bronze
> in their bellies, namely John's.
> — X.J. Kennedy (b. 1929)

> Adam
> Had 'em
> —Anonymous

Although it is a short form, compression is a true art, and the epigram is not the form for everyone. It was the favorite form of J. V. Cunningham. His epigrams show that it is not merely a form for humorous subjects, but can contain the most serious as well:

> I drive Westward. Tumble and loco weed
> Persist. And in the vacancies of need,
> The leisure of desire, whirlwinds a face
> As luminous as love, lost as this place.
> — J.V. Cunningham (1911-1985)

Timothy Steele, in his collection of Cunningham's work, suggests that the conditions of Cunningham's life may very well have influenced the prominence of the epigram in his body of work. He certainly had a natural talent for the pithy form, but perhaps his attention to teaching full-time and publishing prose influenced his form. (See *Writing for Your Life.*)

* * *

- Choose a subject that would benefit from getting right to the point. Make a statement about love. Give advice. Use irony. One common type of epigram presents the poet pretending to be something inanimate, and is often a riddle. (See also the exercises in *Natural Tunes and Inhabitation.*)

Sonnet

The sonnet is a fourteen-line poem, one of the most well-known verse forms. The word *sonnet* comes from the Italian *sonetto*, a little song or sound, which previously came from the Latin *sonus*, meaning sound. It is thought to have been invented by Giacomo de Lentino, around the year 1200.

Many traditional sonnets were written in the meter of iambic pentameter: five feet or ten syllables to every line, with every other syllable stressed. There are different traditional rhyme schemes for the sonnet, the best known being the following:

> Shakespeare: abab cdcd efef gg
> Spenser: ababbcbccdcdee
> Petrarch: abba, abba—with the sestet rhyming cdcdcd,
>   cdecde, cdccdc, or other variations which don't end
>   in a couplet.
> Wordsworth: abbaaccb dedeff

The first eight lines or *octave* of the Petrarchan sonnet presents the theme and develops it. The following sestet reflects upon it in its first three lines and brings it to a close in the final three. The Shakespearian sonnet allows a break between octave and sestet, but is generally composed of three quatrains, each with different pairs of rhymes, and a final couplet with its own rhyme. An important feature of the Shakespearean sonnet is this last couplet, which closes the poem with a climax, or a philosophical reflection on what has been presented. Spenser's form has an octave and a sestet with a final couplet. Many other poets, such as Milton and Wordsworth, have developed other variations of the sonnet.

Sonnets are sometimes written in a *sequence* or cycle. Some of these cycles (such as a crown or garland of sonnets) have a particular number and elaborate structure. The *garland* of sonnets used by several Russian poets, for instance, consists of fifteen poems. They are arranged so that the final sonnet contains only lines repeated from the preceding poems.

WILLIAM SHAKESPEARE (1564-1616)

When, in Disgrace with Fortune and Men's Eyes

When, in disgrace with Fortune and men's eyes,
I all alone beweep my outcast state,
And trouble deaf heaven with my bootless cries,
And look upon myself and curse my fate,
Wishing me like to one more rich in hope,
Featured like him, like him with friends possessed,
Desiring this man's art, and that man's scope,
With what I most enjoy contented least,
Yet in these thoughts myself almost despising,
Haply I think on thee, and then my state,
Like to the lark at break of day arising
From sullen earth, sings hymns at heaven's gate;
For thy sweet love rememb'red such wealth brings
That then I scorn to change my state with kings.

Considering the many sonnets written by such poets as Yeats, Frost, Auden, and Millay to name just a few, one can see that the form has thrived into this century. Many contemporary sonnets are written with different rhyme schemes (or without rhyme), with varying meter, and contain a variety of subjects. The poem below, "At the Mailbox," which, in the first few lines appears to be a love poem, uses the sonnet form to address a lizard. The poem also explores the patterns we might develop and tolerate in our lives.

Marilyn Nelson's "Chosen," uses both exact and slant rhyme and shapes the sonnet into tercets. She uses the form's compression to articulate a terrible incident which has a historical weight. Consider how the following poems both use tradition and bend it, in both the form and choice of subjects.

MARILYN NELSON (b. 1946)

Chosen

Diverne wanted to die, that August night
his face hung over hers, a sweating moon.
She wished so hard, she killed part of her heart.

If she had died, her one begotten son,
her life's one light, would never have been born.
Pomp Atwood might have been another man:

born with a single race, another name.
Diverne might not have known the starburst joy
her son would give her. And the man who came

out of a twelve-room house and ran to her
close shack across three yards that night, to leap
onto her cornshuck pallet. Pomp was their

share of the future. And it wasn't rape.
In spite of her raw terror. And his whip.

DIANE THIEL (b. 1967)

At the Mailbox

The first few times we met, our hearts would rise.
You must have thought that I had no excuse
since I am over a thousand times your size.
But ever since my brother introduced
the two of us, and showed his sibling love,
by catching you to put you in my hair—
I've had the kind that lizards can't get out of.
Now I tap the box to let you know I'm there,
a ritual we both appreciate.
Between my much awaited mail, you leave
your gifts. What would I do, if every day
my little house would open and receive
a mountain, where my living room once stood?
I'd move. At least, I like to think I would.

*   *   *

• Try the sonnet. You could select a rhyme scheme. Or, as you write
    the first few lines, a rhyme scheme may begin to emerge.
    To better understand the form, I encourage you to use
    iambic pentameter (with minimal variations) at first. (See
    The Weave of Meter.) Later, you can experiment with more

174

variations. Though the subject of love often conjures up a sonnet, don't feel limited to this. Consider the startling subjects of the contemporary poems above. Write a poem which addresses another living being, maybe even the tiniest, as "At the Mailbox" does. Or perhaps use the compression of a sonnet to depict a traumatic event, as Marilyn Nelson does. Note, also, Nelson's use of paradox (or contradiction) to deal with the terror. (See "paradox" in *How you Say a Thing*.)

- "Translate" Shakespeare's sonnet into a love poem in contemporary English, or perhaps, a different character's voice. (See also the exercises in *Versions of Translation*.)

Sestina

The word *sestina* comes from the Italian *sesto*, meaning sixth (from the Latin root *sextus*). This form is based on sixes and is an ideal exercise for the mathematical mind. The elaborate repetitions are reminiscent of the patterns we see in the natural world. The form is thought to have been invented in Provence in the thirteenth century by the troubadour poet, Daniel Arnaut. Dante admired Arnaut's poetry and popularized the form by writing sestinas in Italian.

The sestina has six unrhymed stanzas of six lines each, with the end words repeating in a precise pattern throughout the poem. The repeated words create a rhyme-like effect that occurs at seemingly unpredictable intervals as the pattern changes from stanza to stanza. The poem then ends with a three-line stanza, each line containing two of the words:

(ABCDEF/FAEBDC/CFDABE/ECBFAD/DEACFB/BDFECA/AB,CD,EF).

The final poem therefore contains thirty-nine lines made up of 6+6+6+6+6+6+3.

When used to the poem's advantage, the repetitions create a forward movement, and the words serve different functions in the progression of the poem. They might also create a cyclical effect.

Many poets have enjoyed working in the form, including Algernon Charles Swinburne, Rudyard Kipling, Ezra Pound, Elizabeth Bishop, W.H. Auden, Donald Justice, and Mona Van Duyn. Dana Gioia's "My Confessional Sestina" uses the form to make a satirical comment about workshop poems, as well as confessional poetry.

DANA GIOIA (b. 1950)

My Confessional Sestina

Let me confess. I'm sick of these sestinas
written by youngsters in poetry workshops
for the delectation of their fellow students,

and then published in little magazines
that no one reads, not even the contributors
who at least in this omission show some taste.

Is this merely a matter of personal taste?
I don't think so. Most sestinas
are such dull affairs. Just ask the contributors
the last time they finished one outside of a workshop,
even the poignant one on herpes in that new little magazine
edited by their most brilliant fellow student.

Let's be honest. It has become the form for students,
an exercise to build technique rather than taste
and the official entry blank into the little magazines —
because despite its reputation, a passable sestina
isn't very hard to write, even for kids in workshops
who care less about being poets than contributors.

Granted nowadays everyone is a contributor.
My barber is currently a student
in a rigorous correspondence school workshop.
At lesson six he can already taste
success having just placed his own sestina
in a national tonsorial magazine.

Who really cares about most little magazines?
Eventually not even their own contributors
who having published a few preliminary sestinas
send their work East to prove they're no longer students.
They need to be recognized as the new arbiters of taste
so they can teach their own graduate workshops.

Where will it end? The grim cycle of workshops
churning out poems for little magazines
no one honestly finds to their taste?
This ever-lengthening column of contributors
scavenging the land for more students
teaching them to write their boot-camp sestinas?

Perhaps there is an afterlife where all contributors
have two workshops, a tasteful little magazine, and sexy
        students
who worshipfully memorize their every sestina.

* * *

- In a workshop (ignoring Gioia's condemnation for the moment), to make sense of the form, you might write a collective sestina. Choose six words and write them on the board. Set up a "grid" for the poem. Have participants call out lines which end with the appropriate words. Don't expect an exquisite poem to emerge, but it is a fun way to make sense of the form, and some interesting lines will likely appear.

- Though it may be easy to follow the rules and "fill in the blanks" to create a passable sestina, writing a good one is not an easy task. It is definitely not the form for all subjects. Sestinas tend to lag midway, and a good one needs a serious charge or turn of events, perhaps a narrative twist. Try to choose a subject which will have some shift at its center. Another hint is to change the grammar of the chosen words, as in Gioia's use of "taste."

- Adopt (and adapt) six words from a writer who has influenced you. Give credit to your source. Use them to write an "homage," perhaps. Donald Justice did this in his "Sestina on Six Words by Weldon Kees" (see excerpt in *Occasions for Reflection*.)

- Since so many sestinas seem to lag, the form might provide a good opportunity to "invent" a new form. Use the concept and pattern of repetition, but try a half sestina, a *sestria*, perhaps.

- As Gioia does, make a comment about a particular form, using the form. Many writers have done this. Louise Bogan, for instance, in "Single Sonnet," chooses the form of a sonnet to address the "heroic mould of the sonnet."

Villanelle

The word *villanelle* comes from *villanella*—an old Italian folk song. There are six stanzas (5 stanzas of 3 lines and 1 of 4 lines) The first and last lines of the first stanza are repeated throughout the poem—in the intricate pattern of $A^1bA^2/abA^1/abA^2/abA^1/ab$ A^2/abA^1A^2. The poem has a rhyme scheme of aba throughout, with a variation in the last stanza.

The pattern of repetition in the villanelle can create a cyclical, hypnotic effect, like a tide coming back in. The form also reinforces the ideas expressed in the poem.

Elizabeth Bishop's villanelle, "One Art," is a powerful example of the possibilities of the villanelle. In this poem, she is talking about loss, and the poem moves through the different kinds of loss one might experience. The subject is a good one for this form, in which the repetition has a deliberate function. Notice that she does not repeat the A^2 line exactly, but repeats its meaning. She also alters the A^1 line in the last stanza. The variation is enchanting.

ELIZABETH BISHOP (1911-1979)

One Art

The art of losing isn't hard to master;
so many things seem filled with the intent
to be lost that their loss is no disaster.

Lose something every day. Accept the fluster
of lost door keys, the hour badly spent.
The art of losing isn't hard to master.

Then practice losing farther, losing faster:
places, and names, and where it was you meant
to travel. None of these will bring disaster.

I lost my mother's watch. And look! my last, or
next-to-last, of three loved houses went.
The art of losing isn't hard to master.

I lost two cities, lovely ones. And, vaster,
some realms I owned, two rivers, a continent.
I miss them, but it wasn't a disaster.

—Even losing you (the joking voice, a gesture
I love) I shan't have lied. It's evident
the art of losing's not too hard to master
though it may look like (Write it!) like disaster.

As the losses mount in the poem, the voice builds in intensity. Bishop's poem also presents an opportunity to talk about process and revision of a poem, and the development of a thought. Brett C. Millier writes:

> Elizabeth Bishop left seventeen drafts of her poem "One Art" among her papers. In the first draft, she lists all the things she's lost in her life—keys, pens, glasses, cities—and then she writes "one might think this would have prepared me/for losing one average-sized not exceptionally/beautiful or dazzlingly intelligent person.../ But it doesn't seem to have at all..." By the seventeenth draft, nearly every word has been transformed...

The villanelle form can also be an appropriate one to convey an element of humor or irony. Wendy Cope's "Lonely Hearts" uses the villanelle to explore the personal ads, which seem more and more a reality of modern-day life. The form in this poem enhances the subject. The repetition has a distinct purpose here, as does the rhyme. Otherwise, the poem might read as a mere series of ads:

WENDY COPE (b. 1945)

Lonely Hearts

Can someone make my simple wish come true?
Male biker seeks female for touring fun.
Do you live in North London? Is it you?

Gay vegetarian whose friends are few,
I'm into music, Shakespeare and the sun.
Can someone make my simple wish come true?

Executive in search of something new —

Perhaps bisexual woman, arty, young.
Do you live in North London? Is it you?

Successful, straight and solvent? I am too —
Attractive Jewish lady with a son.
Can someone make my simple wish come true?

I'm Libran, inexperienced and blue —
Need slim non-smoker, under twenty-one.
Do you live in North London? Is it you?

Please write (with photo) to Box 152.
Who knows where it may lead once we've begun?
Can someone make my simple wish come true?
Do you live in North London? Is it you?

The villanelle form is a good one as an exercise because it helps to hone the skill of using a repeated line, like the refrain of a song. In a case such as "One Art," it might allow one to explore the many layers which surround a single subject, such as loss. In "Lonely Hearts," the repetition achieves the "listing" effect of newspaper ads, and provides a humorous commentary on how similar all the ads tend to sound.

Other contemporary poets have found the villanelle useful for conveying various subjects. Carolyn Beard Whitlow, for instance, has used the villanelle as a blues poem, another form with a structure of repetition. (See *Crossroads*.)

* * *

• You might choose a subject which has many angles to explore, so the repetition has a purpose and does not become tedious. Allow the form to work for you. Try to create movement within the poem by exploring different layers of meaning in the repeated line or by creating a narrative within.

Rondel, Rondeau and Triolet

The *rondeau* and *rondel* are very similar French forms. The words come from the French *rond*, meaning round, as each line comes round, or is repeated.

The rondeau consists of thirteen lines of three stanzas, the first and last stanza of five lines, the second of three (not including the refrains). There are two rhymes in the poems. The opening words of the first line (or sometimes the whole first line) form unrhymed refrains in the second and third stanzas, often puns. The pattern is: aabba, aabR, aabbaR (the R signifies the refrain).

PAUL LAURENCE DUNBAR (1872-1906)

We Wear the Mask

We wear the mask that grins and lies,
It hides our cheeks and shades our eyes —
This debt we pay to human guile;
With torn and bleeding hearts we smile,
And mouth with myriad subtleties.

Why should the world be over-wise,
In counting all our tears and sighs?
Nay, let them only see us, while
    We wear the mask.

We smile, but O great Christ, our cries
To thee from tortured souls arise.
We sing, but oh the clay is vile
Beneath our feet, and long the mile;
But let the world dream otherwise,
    We wear the mask!

The rondel is a poem of fourteen lines, again using two rhymes and a refrain. The first two lines of the first quatrain occur at the close of the second and concluding stanza. The meter and rhyme scheme may vary, but a typical arrangement is ABba, abAB,

2

abbaAB. The rondel has sometimes been shortened to thirteen lines. Swinburne invented a different "roundel," (Chaucerian spelling), as he termed it, with a structure of three tercets on two rhymes, with a refrain from the opening of the first line rhyming with the second line. The rhyme scheme is thus: abaR, bab, abaR. In the following poem, Swinburne uses the form to illustrate and discuss the roundel:

ALGERNON CHARLES SWINBURNE (1837–1909)

A Roundel is wrought as a ring or a starbright sphere,
With craft of delight and with cunning of sound unsought,
That the heart of the hearer may smile if to pleasure his ear
    A roundel is wrought.

Its jewel of music is carven of all or of aught—
Love, laughter, or mourning—remembrance or rapture or fear—
That fancy may fashion to hang in the ear of thought.

As a bird's quick song runs round, and the hearts in us hear—
Pause answers to pause, and again the same strain caught,
So moves the device whence, round as a pearl or tear,
    A roundel is wrought.

The *triolet* is, essentially, a shorter version of the rondel, popular among French medieval poets such as Eustace Deschamps. It was revived by Jean de la Fontaine in the seventeenth century and into the nineteenth century.

It is another form particularly useful for subjects which contain several angles or layers, or a cyclical quality, such as the following triolet by contemporary Scottish poet Gerry Cambridge. Note, also, the effect of the varying grammar of each line.

GERRY CAMBRIDGE (b. 1959)

Goldfinch in Spring

That finch which sings above my head,
Last year's speckled egg, is now
A partner in some nest instead,
That finch which sings above my head,

Buff-gold dandy masked with red,
And hen on eggs upon some swaying bough
That finch which sings. Above my head
Last year's speckled egg is now.

Frederick Morgan's "1904" is a good example of a variation on the form, where the single repetition enhances the idea of the secret kept for years.

FREDERICK MORGAN (b. 1922)

1904

The things they did together, no one knew
It was late June. Behind the old wood-shed
wild iris was in blossom, white and blue,
but what those proud ones did there, no one knew,
though some suspected there were one or two
who led the others where they would be led.
Years passed—but what they did there, no one knew,
those summer children long since safely dead.

* * *

• Try a triolet, a rondel or rondeau. Choose a subject which might benefit from the reinforcement of a line, like the cycles felt (or heard) in Cambridge's poem or the passage of time in Morgan's poem. Get a handle on each form by trying to adhere to it at first. Later, you can experiment with variations, and use the repetition to its greatest advantage in your particular poem.

Pantoum

The *pantoum*, of Malayan origin, is another form using repetition. Victor Hugo first described the pantoum in the West. It became a popular form (with some variations) among French poets such as Louisa Siefert and Charles Baudelaire. It became prevalent in England in the late nineteenth century, but was not used much in America until the last half of the twentieth century.

The poem is made up of stanzas of four lines: lines two and four of one stanza are repeated as lines one and three of the next. The poem can have any length. Sometimes the final stanza uses the first and third lines of the first stanza as its second and fourth lines. This creates the effect of completion, giving the poem a feeling of having come full circle.

Shirley Geok-lin Lim's poem takes on the heavy subject of Chinese female infanticide as a result of the one child law. The "soot" in the poem refers to a common method of smothering girl children. Of her choice of form for this poem, Lim has stated that she believes poetry must give pleasure and that use of meter and rhyme are ways to enhance the musicality. She believes that sometimes the most terrible subjects might best be cast in language which gives the most pleasure, as if to somehow rise beyond the horror.

SHIRLEY GEOK-LIN LIM (b. 1944)

Pantoum for Chinese Women

> "At present, the phenomenon of butchering, drowning, and leaving to die female infants has been very serious."
>
> (*People's Daily* of Beijing, March 3, 1983)

They say a child with two mouths is no good.
In the slippery wet, a hollow space
Smooth gumming, echoing wide for food.
No wonder my man is not here at his place.

In the slippery wet, a hollow space,
a slit narrowly sheathed within its hood.
No wonder my man is not here at his place:
He is digging for the dragon jar of soot,

that slit, narrowly sheathed within its hood!
His mother, squatting, coughs by the fire's blaze
while he digs for the dragon jar of soot.
We had saved ashes for a hundred days.

His mother, squatting, coughs by the fire's blaze.
The child kicks against me, mewing like a flute.
We had saved ashes for a hundred days,
knowing, if the time came, that we would.

The child kicks against me, crying like a flute
Through its two weak mouths. His mother prays,
Knowing when the time comes, that we would,
For broken clay is never set in glaze.

Through her two weak mouths his mother prays.
She will not pluck the rooster, nor serve its blood,
For broken clay is never set in glaze:
Women are made of river sand and wood.

She will not pluck the rooster nor serve its blood.
My husband frowns, pretending in his haste
Women are made of river sand and wood.
Milk soaks the bedding. I cannot bear the waste.

My husband frowns, pretending in his haste.
Oh clean the girl, dress her in ashy soot!
Milk soaks our bedding. I cannot bear the waste.
They say a child with two mouths is no good.

* * *

• As a pantoum can be of any length, start with a few stanzas. Be
    willing to change your initial lines if you find yourself
    heading in a different direction than you intended—which
    often happens with such a form.

Occasions for Reflection
(Ode, Homage, Epithalamium, Elegy)

Each of these forms is often written for a particular occasion or in
honor of someone or something:

Ode

The ode (from the Greek word *aeidein*, "to sing,") has undergone
many changes throughout history—from the Greek poet Pindar's
victory odes to the Horatian odes, such as those of Alexander
Pope—to irregular odes, such as Keats' "Ode on a Grecian Urn." The
ode is generally considered a lyric poem which addresses someone
or something not present. Pablo Neruda's (1904-1973) "Ode to the
Watermelon" is a good example of the way the form might be used
to talk about an everyday object—and beyond it:

> the coolest of all
> the planets crosses
> the sky,
> the round, magnificent
> star-filled watermelon.
> (translated by Robert Bly)

JOHN KEATS (1795-1821)

Ode on a Grecian Urn

Thou still unravished bride of quietness,
  Thou foster child of silence and slow time,
Sylvan historian, who canst thus express
  A flowery tale more sweetly than our rhyme:
What leaf-fringed legend haunts about thy shape
  Of deities and mortals, or of both,
      In Tempe or the dales of Arcady?
  What men or gods are these? What maidens loth?
What mad pursuit? What struggle to escape?
  What pipes and timbrels? What wild ecstasy?

Heard melodies are sweet, but those unheard
    Are sweeter; therefore, ye soft pipes, play on;
Not to the sensual ear, but, more endeared,
    Pipe to the spirit ditties of no tone:
Fair youth, beneath the trees, thou canst not leave
    Thy song, nor ever can those trees be bare;
        Bold lover, never, never canst thou kiss,
Though winning near the goal—yet, do not grieve;
        She cannot fade, though thou hast not thy bliss
    For ever wilt thou love, and she be fair!

Ah, happy, happy boughs! that cannot shed
    Your leaves, nor ever bid the Spring adieu;
And, happy melodist, unwearièd,
    For ever piping songs for ever new;
More happy love! more happy happy love!
    For ever warm and still to be enjoyed,
        For ever panting and for ever young;
All breathing human passion far above
    That leaves a heart high-sorrowful and cloyed,
        A burning forehead, and a parching tongue.

Who are these coming to the sacrifice?
    To what green altar, O mysterious priest,
Leads't thou that heifer lowing at the skies,
    And all her silken flanks with garlands drest?
What little town by river or sea shore,
    Or mountain-built with peaceful citadel,
        Is emptied of this folk, this pious morn?
And, little town, the streets for evermore
    Will silent be; and not a soul to tell
        Why thou art desolate, can e'er return.

O Attic shape! Fair attitude! with brede
    Of marble men and maidens overwrought,
With forest branches and the trodden weed;
    Thou, silent form, dost tease us out of thought
As doth Eternity: Cold Pastoral!
    When old age shall this generation waste,
        Thou shalt remain, in midst of other woe
    Than ours, a friend to no man, to whom thou say'st,
Beauty is truth, truth beauty,—that is all
        Ye know on earth, and all ye need to know.

Homage

Many poets have written poems in homage of someone or something, in particular in homage to other poets. Often the poem takes the form of a response to a particular line or text. Weldon Kees' "Homage to Arthur Waley" uses the last line of Po Chü-I, translated by Waley:

WELDON KEES (1914-1955)

Homage to Arthur Waley

Seattle weather: it has rained for weeks in this town,
The dampness breeding moths and a gray summer.
I sit in the smoky room reading your book again,
My eyes raw, hearing the trains steaming below me
In the wet yard, and I wonder if you are still alive.
Turning the worn pages, reading once more:
"By misty waters and rainy sands, while the yellow dusk
        thickens."

Many of Donald Justice's (b. 1925) poems declare an influence in the very title: "After a Phrase Abandoned by Wallace Stevens," "Homage to the Memory of Wallace Stevens," "Variations on a Text by Vallejo," or "Sestina on Six Words by Weldon Kees," which begins:

I often wonder about the others
Where they are bound for on the voyage,
What is the reason for their silence,
Was there some reason to go away?
It may be they carry a dark burden,
Expect some harm, or have done harm...

Lucille Clifton's (b. 1936) "Homage to my Hips" is one example of the form which expands the traditional notion of "homage":

they don't fit into little
petty places...
they don't like to be held back.
these hips have never been enslaved...

Epithalamium

An epithalamium, a poem celebrating marriage, comes from the Greek word meaning "upon the bridal chamber." There is no fixed form, but the poem usually tells something about the wedding— about the past of the bride and groom, praises them, and gives blessings. The Greek poet Sappho made the epithalamium a distinct form. In ancient times, it was sung by a chorus outside the couple's bedroom.

> from Andromache's Wedding
>
> Kypros!
> A herald came.
> Idaos. Racing powerfully...
>
> Myrrh and cassia and incense rode on the wind.
> Old women sang happily
> and all the men sang out with thrilling force,
> calling on Paean, great archer, lord of the lyre,
> and sang of Hektor and Andromache like gods.
>   —Sappho (c. 600 BCE)

Some poets have composed their own epithalamiums, one of the most famous being Edmund Spenser's celebration of his own marriage. Spenser was also responsible for the term *prothalamion*, a poem written before the nuptials.

Elegy

The elegy is also an ancient form, the word deriving from the Greek word *elegeia* (song of mourning). The elegy in ancient Greek and Latin was not always "elegiac" in the modern sense. It was any poem in a particular meter—elegiac meter—which consists of a *distich*, or couplet, with one line of classical hexameter (dactylic, six beats) and the second of elegiac pentameter, (five beats) such as the following lines from "Pasa Thalassa Thalassa," from E. A. Robinson:

> Down with a twittering flash go the smooth and inscrutable
>   swallows,
> Down to the place made theirs by the cold work of the sea.

(See *The Weave of Meter.*)

In English, the traditional elegiac stanza is a four-line stanza of iambic pentameter, rhymed abab. However, the elegy has taken on many different forms throughout time and geography.

Among the Romans in the first century, the elegy was mostly used for love poems. John Donne returned to the origins of the form with his funeral elegy, as did German poets Johann Wolfgang Goethe and Friedrich Schiller. American poet Walt Whitman's famous long elegy, "When Lilacs Last in the Dooryard Bloomed" is both a lament and a coming to terms, following the Civil War. German poet Rainer Maria Rilke wrote his famous *Duino Elegies* in 1912, ten poems which reflect on art and death. (See also the excerpt from Shelley's famous elegy for John Keats, "Adonais," in *Stanzas.*)

Clearly, the elegy can have a variety of forms and subjects. Consider Donald Hall's "Names of Horses," which addresses the horses of our history, the burdens they carried, and their often ignoble deaths:

DONALD HALL (b. 1928)

Names of Horses

All winter your brute shoulders strained against collars, padding
and steerhide over the ash hames, to haul
sledges of cordwood for drying through spring and summer,
for the Glenwood stove next winter, and for the simmering
    range.

In April you pulled cartloads of manure to spread on the fields,
dark manure of Holsteins, and knobs of your own clustered with
    oats.
All summer you mowed the grass in meadow and hayfield, the
mowing machine clacketing beside you, while the sun walked
    high in the morning;

and after noon's heat, you pulled a clawed rake through the
    same acres,
gathering stacks, and dragged the wagon from stack to stack,
and the built hayrack back, uphill to the chaffy barn,
three loads of hay a day from standing grass in the morning.

Sundays you trotted the two miles to church with the light load
of a leather quartertop buggy, and grazed in the sound of
    hymns.
Generation on generation, your neck rubbed the windowsill
of the stall, smoothing the wood as the sea smooths glass.

When you were old and lame, when your shoulders hurt
    bending to graze,
one October the man, who fed you and kept you, and harnessed
    you every morning,
led you through corn stubble to sandy ground above Eagle Pond,
and dug a hole beside you where you stood shuddering in your
    skin,

and lay the shotgun's muzzle in the boneless hollow behind
    your ear,
and fired the slug into your brain, and felled you into your grave,
shoveling sand to cover you, setting goldenrod upright above
    you,
where by next summer a dent in the ground made your
    monument.

For a hundred and fifty years, in the pasture of dead horses,
roots of pine trees pushed through the pale curves of your ribs,
yellow blossoms flourished above you in autumn, and in winter
frost heaved your bones in the ground—old toilers, soil makers:

O Roger, Mackerel, Riley, Ned, Nellie, Chester, Lady Ghost.

*   *   *

- Try an ode, homage, epithalamium, or elegy, depending on which
  meets the present conditions of your life.

- For the ode, try addressing a piece of art, as Keats does in "Ode on
  a Grecian Urn." In workshops, I have sometimes brought
  in photographs of Grecian urns, sometimes with
  translations of their distinctive inscriptions, to give an idea
  of the kind of art which inspired Keats' poem. (See *Art
  Speaks.*)

- For the ode or homage, perhaps take a lead from Neruda's "Ode to the Watermelon" or Lucille Clifton's "Homage to my Hips" and choose an everyday object. Young children find this a fun exercise:

  Homage to my Mouth

  This mouth is a big mouth.
  My dad says it has a motor.
  If I had no mouth I could not talk
  and talk some more and talk some more,
  so I give homage to my very big great mouth.
  　　　—Keith Philips, 4th grade

- Write an homage to a writer who has influenced you. Reflect on a line or idea which has always remained with you. Declare your source of inspiration in the title, within the piece, or as an epigraph perhaps.

- An elegy might be an occasion for reflection on a recent or not-so-recent loss. Consider the way Hall addresses the horses in the above poem. Write an elegy for something non-human which has been lost, perhaps directly addressing the animal, plant, idea, etc. (See also *Dear Star, Do you Know the Moon?*)

Haiku, Tanka, Renga

Japanese forms have also found their way into English poetry. For over a thousand years, tanka have been written: five line poems with thirty-one syllables, following the pattern 5,7,5,7,7. The popular haiku (which means "beginning verse" in Japanese) derives from the first lines of tanka. The haiku, a poem of seventeen syllables (5,7,5) often depicts something in nature, but carries in its compressed style a mystical suggestion of other interpretations. It is important to note, however, that the Japanese syllable is quite a different entity than the English syllable. Therefore, an English haiku need not necessarily have seventeen syllables, but rather three short lines. The poem might have one of many tones, from somber to humorous. The most important thing is the leap contained in the poem's compression. The poem should reverberate.

MATSUO BASHO (1644-1694)

Under cherry trees
Soup, the salad, fish, and all...
Seasoned with petals.

KOBAYASHI ISSA (1763-1827)

Cricket, be
careful! I'm rolling
over!
            —trans. Robert Bly

Haiku (or hokku) were also used as the first three lines for a series of tanka called *renga*. Renga were often collaborative poems, and many Japanese poets wrote books of rules for the form. Each stanza would connect to the previous one (through an image, perhaps, or a play on words), but not to the stanza before. The rules would also describe the pacing from beginning to end. The first six or eight stanzas would set up the poem. The middle stanzas would become quite elaborate, include humor and move through a great range of subjects and emotions. The final six or eight stanzas would move quickly—with rapid, closely related images like simple farewells at the end of a gathering. Often the final stanza would contain an image of spring, indicating hope and rejuvenation. Traditionally, Japanese renga might involve over two hundred poets writing a single poem.

Matsuo Basho, considered one of the great writers of haiku, preferred renga of thirty-six stanzas. He spoke of the linking technique as having the essential quality of *hibiki*, or echo. He believed that the second stanza should echo the first, via a thread of connection, as in the following (the poem need not rhyme, of course, although the following translation does):

MATSUO BASHO (1644-1694)

From this day on,
I will be known as a wanderer
leaving in morning showers.

You will sleep your nights
Nestled among sasanqua flowers.
　　　　—trans. Diane Thiel

Basho is known also for his travelogues—which were written as a mosaic of prose and poetry, and which often contained linked poems, the parts often identified as "written by host" or "written by guest," a kind of call and response.

Japanese forms have been much revived in contemporary verse, and have often been used in innovative ways. W.H. Auden's "Elegy for JFK," for instance, is formally intriguing in its use of a series of haiku. And many poets, such as Mexican poet Octavio Paz, have revived the tradition of collaborative renga, with one poet producing the first three lines and another, the following two.

* * *

• Try haiku and tanka. In a group setting, you might revive the ancient tradition of renga and attempt poems in collaboration. The first person should write the first poem of three lines, the next of two lines, the following, again of three lines, as discussed above.

• Just for fun, you might try the types of links discussed in the exercises in *The Man-Moth* to see what kind of "accidental" connections arise. Write your tanka (or haiku) individually, but read them as if they were a renga written in collaboration. See what mysterious echoes appear.

Ghazal

The ghazal (pronounced *ghuzzle*—with the *gh* in the throat like the French *r*) is an ancient Persian form which also became popular in India. Hafiz (1325-1389) is considered the master of the ghazal, although many Persian poets, such as Rumi, Jami, and Sanai also composed many ghazals. Ghalib (1797-1869) is generally considered the master of the form in Urdu (the youngest of the many languages of India).

The ghazal contains a series of couplets—each its own entity, but connected by the leap the mind takes via the disunity. Although the ghazal receives its name from a word which means "sweet talk," or talk for a beloved, the loved one is often a mystical beloved. The couplets often contain an element of longing:

> When your devotee's condition alters but a little,
> Life presents itself to me with another cup of sorrow.
>
> Your remembrance is sewn to the hem of my heart
> No matter where I go, I cannot forget my sorrow.
> —Darshan Singh (1921-1987)

According to Dr. Vinod Sena of Delhi University, the term also derives from the same root as the word *gazelle*. Sena likens the couplet of the ghazal with the final couplet of the Shakepearean sonnet:

> Just as a deer in the forest bounds from place to place, likewise the form of lyric poetry known as the ghazal is expected to have that same bounce...So it bounds from one verse to another, and each such verse or couplet is a world of meaning unto itself....The Shakespearian couplet seems to sum up the essence of whatever has gone before in a Shakespearean sonnet. Imagine a series of such couplets with that same intensity and completeness of meaning in each making up a single poem. Nine such verses would be like nine Shakespearean sonnets compressed into nine couplets.

The traditional Persian form had a precise metrical and rhyming structure, but the meter does not have an English equivalent. The opening couplet (*matla*) rhymes and sets up the structure for the poem—the rhyme scheme (*qafi*) and the refrain (*radif*). To best approximate the traditional Persian form, each of the lines should contain the same number of syllables, although some poets operate on a principle of accents per line, rather than syllable count.

The form first became known in Europe in the early 1800's with a German translation of Hafiz. Goethe modeled Hafiz in his *West-Eastern Divan*. The following translation of one of Hafiz's many ghazals, by H. Wilberforce Clarke, does not have a consistent syllable count, but it does show the pattern of repetition at the end of each couplet. Certain images appear often in traditional ghazals, such as wine, tears, the cup, the cup-bearer, the tavern, the beloved. The many symbols of intoxication refer to the intoxication of love or grace. One of the elements of the form is its use of this tradition of images in new patterns. Each image may have many meanings. Much may be lost in translation, however, as only one sense of the word is often conveyed.

HAFIZ   (c. 1320-c.1390)

If from the rock in Badakhshan, the ruby will come forth.
From the mountain gorge, like sugar, the water of the Rukni,
    will come forth.

Within the city of Shiraz, from the door of every house,
A heart-ravisher, lovely, graceful, will come forth.

From the dwelling of the kazi, of the mufti, of the shaikh, and of
    the muhtasib,
Unalloyed wine, rose of hue, will come forth.

On the pulpit, at the time of ecstasy, and of the manifestation of
    hypocrisy,
From the top of the admonisher's turban, "bang," will come
    forth.

Within the garden, morn and eve, with the voice of the minstrel,
The lament of the bulbul with the twang of the harp will come
    forth.

In such a city (of love's tumult), in separation from the beloved,
    and in grief for separation,
From his dwelling, (O wonder) Hafiz, straight of heart, will come
    forth.

The ghazal sometimes contains a *makhta* (signature couplet with the poet's name) as the final couplet, as in Hafiz's example above. This signature might take many forms. Agha Shahid Ali, for instance, chooses to define his name in a final couplet:

They ask me to tell them what "Shahid" means —
Listen: it means "The Beloved" in Persian, "witness" in Arabic.

John Hollander's ghazal in *Rhyme's Reason* uses the traditional pattern of the ghazal in a poem which clarifies the requirements for the traditional form quite well.

For couplets the ghazal is prime; at the end
Of each one's a refrain like a chime: "at the end."

The recurring rhyme and refrain give the thematically independent couplets an undercurrent of unity:

Two frail arms of your delicate form I pursue,
Inaccessible, vibrant, sublime at the end...

Each new couplet's a different ascent: no great peak
But a low hill quite easy to climb at the end.

Hollander closes his ghazal with a signature, but gives himself the pseudonym Qafia Radif, the terms for the rhyme scheme and refrain of a ghazal.

Now Qafia Radif has grown weary, like life,
At the game he's been wasting his time at. THE END.

Although some poets have written unrhymed ghazals, others such as Agha Shahid Ali encourage a more faithful return to the traditional form of the poem, in order to create the unity within the disunity. Ali comments that "because of Urdu's quantitative syllables and meters, a ghazal usually seems to have the same number of syllables per line when recited or sung." However, one might choose to vary the syllable count and choice of meter. Hollander, for instance, uses mostly anapestic meter, but occasionally varies it with iambic meter (See *The Weave of Meter.*)

At a *mushaira*, a Persian poetry gathering, when the poet recites the first line, sometimes his listeners will recite it back. There is a call and response inherent in the poem's structure as well as in the musicality of its rhyme scheme and repetition. The refrain sets up an expectation for the listener, and an excitement to hear how the next couplet will use the final words. Listeners will sometimes break into the known refrain before the couplet is even completed.

* * *

• Try both an unrhymed ghazal, as well as the traditional form of the ghazal, using the rhyme and refrain.

• To spark your mind, you might use the results from the "random" exercises in the chapter *The Man-Moth*. Note how the series of "if-then, why-because" responses (on the surface disconnected) have an undercurrent of unity.

• In a workshop, you could write a communal ghazal. Write the first couplet together. Decide on a pattern, and then each person write a couplet. Read the couplets out loud—as a single ghazal.

• In a workshop, read ghazals aloud, with audience participation, in the tradition of the mushaira.

Acrostic

The acrostic originated in ancient times. Some of the Hebrew psalms of the Bible are acrostics. The word derives from the Greek *acros* (outermost) and *stichos* (line of poetry). In an acrostic, the letters of the lines spell a vertical word, or group of words. A double acrostic has two vertical arrangements in the middle or at the end of the line. And a (rare) triple acrostic has three vertical arrangements.

The acrostic has been enjoyed over time as a game—from the Greeks to Boccaccio to Chaucer to Edgar Allen Poe. Some years ago, I lived in an old church rectory next to a graveyard in Providence, Rhode Island. As the local lore had it, it was the site where Edgar Allen Poe used to meet his beloved, Sarah Helen Whitman. Years later, H.P. Lovecraft used to meet his friends at the same graveyard and write rhymed acrostics containing the name of Edgar Allen Poe.

Now, you don't necessarily need a graveyard or a writer of influence to inspire an acrostic, but the form, in its design, does seem to contain a secret or riddle. Often it carries the name of a beloved, as in Dave Mason's "Acrostic from Aegina:"

DAVID MASON (b. 1954)

Acrostic from Aegina

Anemones you brought back from the path
Nod in a glass beside our rumpled bed.
Now you are far away. In the aftermath
Even these flowers arouse my sleepy head.

Love, when I think of the ready look in your eyes,
Erotas that would make these stone walls blush
Nerves me to write away the morning's hush.
Nadir of longing, and the red anemones
Over the lucent rim—my poor designs,
X-rated praise I've hidden between these lines.

In this way, with its hidden word or message, the acrostic can have a kind of subversive quality. Mason names his poem as an acrostic, but sometimes, the acrostic is even further concealed. *The New Yorker*, for instance, once unknowingly published an acrostic which named and insulted a prominent anthologist. There is, in fact, a tradition of the insult poem, which makes use of humor and exaggeration and often contains an element of "call and response," as one might imagine—a trading of insults. The epigram has also been a popular form for this type of poem. (See X. J. Kennedy's *Tygers of Wrath: Poems of Hate, Anger, and Invective.*)

Consider also Phillis Levin's "Brief Bio," in which the word that is formed vertically answers the riddle. It would be easy to miss the acrostic nature of this poem:

PHILLIS LEVIN (b. 1954)

Brief Bio

Bearer of no news
Under the sun, except
The spring, I quicken
Time, drawing you to see
Earth's lightest pamphlet,
Reeling mosaic of rainbow dust,
Filament hinging a new set of wings,
Lord of no land, subject to flowers and wind,
Yesterday born in a palace that hangs by a thread.

* * *

• Write an acrostic:
       1. with the name of your beloved
       2. in the tradition of the insult poem
       3. honoring or dishonoring a person in history
       4. as a riddle

Choose a subject that would truly benefit from the "secret message" nature of the poem.

• Try an *abecedarian*, a variant of an acrostic. In this form, each line begins with a letter of the alphabet, in order.

Light Verse
(Limerick, Clerihew, Double Dactyl)

These three forms usually contain light verse. We are all familiar with the limerick, made popular by Edward Lear. The form contains three long and two short lines rhyming aabba and usually has a bawdy subject. The rhymes are often more oral than written, as in *pursued her* and *barracuda* in the following:

> There was a young man from Tahiti
> who went for a swim with his sweetie,
> and as he pursued her,
> a blind barracuda
> ran off with his masculinity.
> —Anonymous

The following example describes the form and its limits quite well:

> A limerick packs laughs anatomical
> Into space that is quite economical.
> But the good ones I've seen
> So seldom are clean,
> And the clean ones so seldom are comical.
> —Anonymous

The clerihew, invented by Edmund Clerihew Bentley (1875-1956), contains two mismatched couplets, one of which contains the name and element of biography of someone as one of the rhymes. At a recent writing conference, R.S. Gwynn immortalized a large percentage of conference participants by writing clerihews with their names. He assumed the *nom de plume*, Clara Hughes, for the act:

> Diane Thiel
> says it's unreal
> how sticky and clammy
> it gets in Miami.
> —Clara Hughes

A particular favorite of mine was the one he wrote for David Mason because of the aural joke in rhyming "naiad" with the

Southern drawl of "bad...."

> David Mason
> was last seen chasin'
> an Aegean naiad.
> He's so bad.

The double dactyl was originated by poet Anthony Hecht (b. 1923). The form has two quatrains, with the last lines of each rhyming. The first three lines of each quatrain have two full dactyls: stressed, unstressed, unstressed. (See *The Weave of Meter.*) The last lines of each quatrain have a meter of stressed, unstressed, unstressed, stressed. Somewhere in the poem, usually in the sixth line, there has to be a single double-dactyl word, such as "gubernatorial" or "incomprehensible":

> PAUL PASCAL (b. 1925)
>
> Tact
>
> Patty-cake, patty cake
> Marcus Antonius,
> What do you think of the
> African Queen?
>
> Gubernatorial
> Duties require my
> Presence in Egypt. Ya
> know what I mean?

* * *

• Trying your hand at these forms can be great fun and make for good challenges. I've noticed that clerihews work particularly well with children. But given the right subject and touch, each of these forms might even rise above the name of light verse, or rather, give light verse a better name.

Crossroads (Blues Poems)

Blues poetry had its roots in music, and in the experience of African Americans. The earliest forms were the work songs, the call and response from one person to another working in the field. These are often referred to as "field hollers." The songs were sometimes secret messages passed back and forth. Slaves were often silenced for fear of the subversive nature of their songs.

Blues poetry emerged from blues music, via such poets as Langston Hughes and Sterling Brown. Although "the blues" is traditionally associated with painful experience, it also has as its center the idea of the triumph of the human spirit.

Some blues poetry adheres to no particular form but is considered blues because of its content. Some has both the content and structure of repetition which old blues songs contain. The traditional blues stanza had three lines, with the first line repeated (with variations) in the second line, and then a third rhyming line. Some blues songs have a structure of four lines.

> In the evenin', in the evenin', momma, when the sun go down,
> In the evenin', darlin' I declare, when the sun go down,
> Yes it's so lonesome, so lonesome, when the one you love is not around.
> —Traditional

> I woke up this mornin' feelin' round for my shoes
> I know about that I got these old walkin' blues
> I woke up this mornin' feelin' round for my shoes
> I know about that, I got them old walkin' blues
> —Robert Johnson

Some contemporary poets have used the blues tradition in innovative ways. Carolyn B. Whitlow, for instance, writes the following blues poem in the form of a villanelle (see *Villanelle.*)

CAROLYN BEARD WHITLOW (b. 1945)

Rockin' a Man, Stone Blind

Cake in the oven, clothes out on the line,
Night wind blowin' against sweet, yellow thighs,
Two-eyed woman rockin' a man stone blind.

Man smell of honey, dark like coffee grind;
Countin' on his fingers since last July.
Cake in the oven, clothes out on the line.

Mister Jacobs say he be colorblind,
But got to tighten belts and loosen ties.
Two-eyed woman rockin' a man stone blind.

Winter becoming angry, rent behind.
Strapping spring sun needed to make mud pies.
Cake in the oven, clothes out on the line.

Looked in the mirror, Bessie's face I find.
I be so down low, my man be so high.
Two-eyed woman rockin' a man stone blind.

Policemans found him; damn near lost my mind.
Can't afford no flowers; can't even cry.
Cake in the oven, clothes out on the line.
Two-eyed woman rockin' a man stone blind.

Many of us, when we compare our lives to conditions in other eras or geographies, might feel that we can't possibly be true to the blues, which emerged out of such tremendous human suffering. This kind of poem might provoke some unmasking, or some serious thought about the conditions of our lives (and possibly about our apathy). But we all have cultural and historical memory we can access.

The persistent problems of human society—war, oppression, cruelty to human beings as well as animals—can be subjects one might draw upon as inspiration for the blues. Poems about such universal conditions might have the power to open up our minds to the enduring questions about human existence.

Be true to your sorrow, or the sorrows you feel around you in the world. Singing them out can be one way of addressing them. Doing this exercise in workshops might produce some serious blues poems, or it might be a forum for participants to find out their concerns.

* * *

- Listen to blues music before you write. You might try Robert Johnson, Blind Lemon Jefferson, or Lightnin' Hopkins, to name a few.

- Write a blues poem. What is your deepest sorrow? There is a repeated motif in the blues tradition of meeting the devil at the crossroads. You might write about your own such "encounter," a crossroads of your own life. Try the structure of repetition.

- One variation on this assignment might be to write from someone else's perspective. Think of someone who has undergone something very difficult, and write from that perspective.

- With young children, this exercise often yields somewhat light-hearted responses, but some are quite true to the blues representing the triumph of the human spirit, as in the following poem, "Riding Blues."

  Riding Blues

  When I ride my horse,
  I always fall down.
  When I ride my bike,
  I always fall down,
  But when I ride my dragon,
  I never fall down.
  —Dominique Flores, 3rd grade, Kinloch Park

  Monster Blues

  I got the monster blues.
  Because my monster bothers me a lot.
  He doesn't let me do my homework.
  — Vanesa Veloso, 3rd grade

Homework Blues

I woke up in the morning.
I woke up in the morning.
I brushed my hair.
I brushed my hair.
I checked my homework.
I checked my homework.
But it wasn't there.
But it wasn't there.
That's my homework blues.
      —Christopher Fils-Aimé, 4th grade

Shipwrecked Blues

I got the can't think
of anything to write blues.
I got the blues.
I am a wreck.
I'm hitting the deck.
I have no clues
I'm thinking, thinking, thinking
I'm on a boat,
that's not afloat.
I'm sinking, sinking, sinking.
I got the blues.
      —Philip Farro, 5th grade

Decision Blues

I've got the decision blues
Whether to say yes or no
To go out or stay in
Whether or not to kiss him
These are the decision blues
To be or not to be
To go or not to go
To or not to, I don't know
These are the horrible d-blues
I've got the d-blues, the d-blues, the d-blues
      —Elizabeth Ogunlade, 8th grade

Ballad and Ballade

Both the ballad and the ballade express the tradition of the link between poetry, story and song, although they are rather different forms.

The ballade is one of the French forms. Some of the greatest inventors of form were the troubadour poets of Southern France, who flourished between the eleventh and thirteenth centuries. The poets sought patrons among the nobility, although occasionally, members of the nobility, for instance, Richard the Lion-Hearted, were troubadours themselves. Troubadours would often travel with apprentices or *jongleurs*, who would accompany the poems with music.

The ballade (from an old French word meaning "dancing song") was a popular troubadour form, usually following the pattern of three stanzas of eight lines each. The form continued to be popular in fourteenth and fifteenth century France, with such poets as Charles d'Orleans, Christine de Pisan and François Villon. The rhyme scheme is ababbcbC (the capital C denotes a line which is repeated at the end of each of the three stanzas). The whole poem thus follows the pattern of: ababbcbC ababbcbC ababbcbC bcbC. There are some variations on the form. The stanza has sometimes consisted of ten lines, where a D would be added. The ballade has often been addressed to a specific person or was written for a particular occasion. It has not been used very widely in English, possibly due to the intricate rhyme scheme, although some poets found the form appropriate for certain subjects.

Geoffrey Chaucer (considered the first great poet of English), poor in his old age, sent the following ballade to his new king, Henry IV, entreating more funds. The king must have appreciated the poem, as he raised Chaucer's pension soon after. "The Complaint of Chaucer to His Purse" is written in middle English, but with a few words clarified, can be readily understood, as can the somewhat exaggerated lament for more money.

GEOFFREY CHAUCER (c.1340-1400)

The Complaint of Chaucer to His Purse

To yow, my purse, and to noon other wight°   person
Complayne I, for ye be my lady dere!
I am so sory, now that ye be lyght;
For certes,° but° ye make me heavy chere,   surely   unless
Me were as leef° be layd upon my bere;   I would like to be
For which unto your mercy thus I crye:
Beth hevy ageyn, or elles moote° I dye!   must

Now voucheth sauf° this day, or° yt be nyght,   vouchsafe   before
That I of yow the blisful soun° may here,   sound
Or see your colour lyk the sonne bryght,
That of yelownesse hadde never pere.
Ye be my lyf, ye be myn hertes stere,°   guide
Quene of comfort and of good companye:
Beth hevy ageyn, or elles moote I dye!

Now purse, that ben to me my lyves lyght
And saveour, as° doun in this world here,   while
Out of this toune helpe me thurgh your myght,
Syn that ye wole nat ben my tresorere;
For I am shave as nye° as any frere.°   close   friar
But yet I pray unto your curtesye:
Beth heavy ageyn, or elles moote I dye!

L'envoy de Chaucer:
O conqueror of Brutes° Albyon,°   Brutus's   England
Which that by lyne and free eleccion
Been verray° kyng, this song to yow I sende;   true
And ye, that mowen° alle our harmes amende,   can
Have mynde upon my supplicacion!

The ballad has been traditionally used for the purpose of story-telling and has quite a different basic structure from the ballade. Any narrative song might be called a ballad. Traditionally, ballads would shift and change as they traveled from place to place. Sir Walter Scott, a renowned collector of Scottish folk ballads, angered a few of his sources by the act. One woman said to him, "They were made for singing and no' for reading, but ye ha'e broken the charm now and they'll never be sung mair." Perhaps something of the oral tradition does get lost in the act of transcribing a ballad—it freezes it in time. On the other hand, the transcribers of ballads and other forms of folklore certainly preserved much of our culture which would have otherwise been lost.

Ballad meter varies, but the traditional ballad stanza is four lines rhymed abcb or abab, with alternating beats of 4,3,4,3. If the feet are iambic, the quatrain is said to have common measure, as in eighteenth century English hymnist John Newton's, "Amazing Grace":

> Amazing grace! how sweet the sound
> That saved a wretch like me!
> I once was lost, but now am found,
> Was blind, but now I see.

The ballad has often been used as a form to convey historical events, and has been adopted by contemporary writers for this purpose, as in Dudley Randall's "Ballad of Birmingham," about the bombing of a church in Birmingham, Alabama in 1963. The ballad shows the shock of the bombing via a mother's efforts, in vain, to keep her daughter safe by keeping her away from the protests and in the church instead:

> The mother smiled to know her child
> Was in the sacred place.
> But that smile was the last smile
> To come upon her face.
>
> For when she heard the explosion,
> Her eyes grew wet and wild.
> She raced through the streets of Birmingham
> Calling for her child.

The subject matter of the ballad has ranged from the comic and irreverent to a very serious and poignant depiction of events, as in Randall's poem discussed above. Walter de la Mare's ballad, "The Listeners," has a very serious tone, although what exactly has happened remains somewhat open to interpretation:

WALTER DE LA MARE (1873–1953)

The Listeners

"Is there anybody there?" said the Traveler,
      Knocking on the moonlit door;
And his horse in the silence champed the grasses
      Of the forest's ferny floor:
And a bird flew up out of the turret,
      Above the Traveler's head:
And he smote upon the door again a second time;
      "Is there anybody there?" he said.
But no one descended to the Traveler;
      No head from the leaf-fringed sill
Leaned over and looked into his gray eyes,
      Where he stood perplexed and still.
But only a host of phantom listeners
      That dwelt in the lone house then
Stood listening in the quiet of the moonlight
      To that voice from the world of men:
Stood thronging the faint moonbeams on the dark stair,
      That goes down to the empty hall,
Hearkening in an air stirred and shaken
      By the lonely Traveler's call.
And he felt in his heart their strangeness,
      Their stillness answering his cry,
While his horse moved, cropping the dark turf,
      'Neath the starred and leafy sky;
For he suddenly smote on the door, even
      Louder, and lifted his head:—
"Tell them I came, and no one answered,
      That I kept my word," he said.
Never the least stir made the listeners,
      Though every word he spake
Fell echoing through the shadowiness of the still house
      From the one man left awake:
Ay, they heard his foot upon the stirrup,
      And the sound of iron on stone,
And how the silence surged softly backward,
      When the plunging hoofs were gone.

*   *   *

- Write a ballad which explores what has happened in "The Listeners," perhaps addressing the event which led to the Traveler's promise. Or, address the reasons why there are only "phantom listeners" in the house.

- I have encountered the following exercise in several workshops over the years:

  Ballad scholar Albert B. Friedman has said that the events of ballads are frequently "the stuff of tabloid journalism—sensational tales of lust, revenge and domestic crime." Use a tabloid newspaper to select subjects for your ballads. (In all honesty, you could probably use any newspaper, considering the nature of much of today's sensationalism in the everyday news.)

- The subject matter of Chaucer's hyperbolic ballade transcends time and almost asks to be "spoofed." Write a modern imitation of the poem, requesting money from parents, a boss, a governmental organization, etc. (See also the exercise with Shakespeare in *Sonnet* and with Poe in *Versions of Translation* for other suggestions for modernizations.)

(See also *Orchestrations.*)

Storytelling and Myth-Making

Although the other sections in this book address elements of myth and storytelling as well, the exercises included here can be used particularly to inspire narrative. Though some of us might not think of ourselves as storytellers, we all are. When something exciting happens, we all have that urge to tell the story. The exercises in this section speak to this impulse and to the idea of archetype and lineage—that we are a continuation of one long story.

Time's Arrow

The physicist, Stephen Hawking, has suggested that if there is no boundary condition for the universe, the arrows of time will not point in the same direction for the whole history of the cosmos. At some point, he theorizes, the universe will begin to contract, and time as we know it will move backwards.

Martin Amis' book, *Time's Arrow,* uses Hawking's idea to explore questions of time. He narrates a life story backwards, with a soul trying to make sense of a backwards world. In doing so, he comments satirically about society—from the weighty and grave to the comic and irreverent. The following passage from the novel describes rain, lightning, and earthquakes from a backwards perspective:

> I know I live on a fierce and magical planet, which sheds or surrenders rain or even flings it off in whipstroke after whipstroke, which fires out bolts of electric gold into the firmament at 186,000 miles per second, which with a single shrug of its tectonic plates can erect a city in half an hour. Creation...is easy, is quick.

The conversations in the book, too, are backwards:

> "Don't go— please."
> "Goodbye, Tod."
> "Don't go."
> "It's no good."
> "Please."
> "There's no future for us."
> Which I greet, I confess, with a silent "Yeah, yeah." Tod resumes:
> "Elsa," he says, "or Rosemary or Juanita or Betty-Jean. You're very special to me."
> "Like hell."
> "But I love you."
> "I can't look you in the eye."

I have noticed in the past, of course that most conversations

would make much better sense if you ran them backward. But with this man-woman stuff, you could run them any way you liked—and still get no further forward.
—Martin Amis (b. 1949)

W. S. Merwin's "Unchopping a Tree" creates a similar effect. In the description of the mammals, the nests, the insects which would have to be returned, the splintered trunk reconnected, one senses the enormity of the destruction in the felling of a single tree. In describing the process backwards, he makes a comment about the intricate balance of nature which, once destroyed, is impossible to restore:

> It goes without saying that if the tree was hollow in whole or in part, and contained old nests of bird or mammal or insect, or hoards of nuts or such structures as wasps or bees build for their survival, the contents will have to be repaired where necessary and reassembled, insofar as possible, in their original order, including the shell of nuts already opened. With spider's webs you must simply do the best you can. We do not have the spider's weaving equipment, nor any substitute for the leaf's living bond with its point of attachment and nourishment.
> — W. S. Merwin (b. 1927)

* * *

• Describe something backwards, Create your reverse-time version in order to make a comment about something that has been done, that might be better undone (e.g., undevelop a new development, unpollute a river, etc.). (See *Going to the Source*.)

Bottle, Baseball, Bra

There are a variety of exercises one can do with objects—in a workshop or on your own. Objects tend to suggest stories, particularly a series of objects. One intriguing approach is to focus on the object as though you had never seen it before. Think, for instance, of the Botswana tribesman in the comic film, *The Gods Must Be Crazy*, who comes upon a coke bottle which has fallen from the sky. The tribe sees the object as sacred.

The objects you choose might be both familiar and unfamiliar. A friend joined me in a workshop I was teaching one day, where we planned to do this exercise. As we assembled a motley assortment of articles in preparation for class, she suggested we bring along an old bra. The students had a laugh, and it became one of the favorite items to write about. The object carried far more significance than we might have predicted. People wrote about the embarrassment of their first bra experiences, for instance:

> My first bra had a bow in the middle, right about where I was supposed to have cleavage. I didn't, of course, since I was only twelve. I didn't really want to start wearing a bra, but I went out and bought one because, at the time, the boys would go around and snap the girls' bra straps. I was petrified that Steve Hinson would reach for mine and wouldn't find one. Then he would know I was flat. After I got one, I was confident. I would even carry my backpack in the front and leave my back free for any thrill-seeking seventh grade boy to grab. But no boys ever did snap my bra...
> —Alessandra Gherardi, FIU

After the workshop, I was bequeathed the old bra—so I could use it as a not-so-personal object in future workshops.

* * *

• Write about a memory (or memories) an object evokes.

• Look at a familiar object with new eyes. Describe the object as though you had never seen it before.

- Find an unfamiliar object and describe it. You might exchange objects with a friend, or someone in a workshop or writer's group. You might also create a myth or story to accompany it. What magical powers does it possess?

- Select a series of objects and construct a narrative. In a workshop, have everyone bring in three objects and then place them together on a table in the room. Each person then selects three objects and writes a short vignette which contains each object (familiar or unfamiliar) in a significant way.

(See *Feelers First*.)

Anonymous Album

Looking at photographs can be inspiring—old photographs of relatives, pictures from childhood. You can find many layers of stories in the moments of your family's history captured on film. Choose an old family photograph to do the exercises below. Preferably, choose a family member you know little about.

Then bring the photograph into a workshop to exchange. Do the same exercises with someone else's photograph. Writing about someone else's photographs might yield particularly interesting results, because you will have fewer preconceptions.

When doing these exercises, you need not be constrained by the photograph. Your response does not have to make reference to the photograph or be limited to the moment or events surrounding the taking of the picture.

The following exercises contain excerpts from in-class responses, some of which inspired longer pieces.

*   *   *

• Write a "photograph in words."

> Red, blue, and gold
> as she stands barefoot in the sand...
> hands raised to a clear sky.
> A floating crimson scarf
> rides the breeze above her head...
> —Cris Farinas, FIU

• Write a dramatic monologue from the perspective of someone in the photograph. Include the setting somehow. (See *Inhabitation.*)

> ...I mean, the alligator farm is cool kind of scary, but boring after half an hour. I hope we get to go to Universal Studios later and see some really cool stuff...My Dad—look at him. He loves taking pictures of us. Probably so that when we grow up, he can bring out the old pictures and embarrass us.
> —Jose Torres, FIU

• What is happening outside the frame of the photo?

> Upon the sight of the formation of the tornado, the actors began shrieking and running towards safety. Cars stopped on the highway. Storm chasers were seeking every possible route to get as close as possible, while clicking their cameras at every conceivable angle...
> —Beth Chiofalo, FIU

• Write about an inanimate object in the picture: This might provide a new thought, or bring back a story which may have nothing to do with the picture.

> Looking at this ornate, heirloom bridal gown, it's hard to believe that it carries the dreaded Klotchnick family curse. Three generations that descended from that Ukrainian matchmaker and part-time psychic, Kvech Klotchnick, have suffered public humiliation when wearing the gown. Perhaps the problem is with Kvech's genes and not the sequined satin outfit itself. Legend has it that marauding Cossacks retreated in disarray when beholding Kvech and her sisters.
>
> As an amateurish psychic, Kvech stubbornly supported Czar Nicholas during the October Revolution. She narrowly escaped the Bolsheviks with her life, emigrating to the New World disguised as the Czarina.
>
> Klotchnick descendants have come and gone. Mysteriously, the lace-appliqued outfit hasn't aged one day. Kvech unintentionally passed it on to her daughter, Sharon. Sharon passed it on to her daughter, Elissa. The pearl-studded dress with its streaming rosette-speckled train has the supernatural power of diverting well-intentioned grooms away from their marriage vows at the last moment.
> — Fred Sherman, UM

• You might also construct a narrative combining elements from the results of all of these exercises.

Scrambled Elements

The mind searches for ways to make sense of disparate elements, to make narrative. Although the following exercise might not always yield the best story, it is a good challenge, and the mere combinations alone often make for good humor: Napoleon, in class, stage fright; Madonna, Buckingham Palace, UFO sighting. The combinations which arise can be kernels of later, more substantial pieces.

* * *

• Have each person write down a character, a place, and an event on three separate scraps of paper. Collect them in piles. Then each participant will select one from each pile. Construct a short narrative using the three elements you have chosen. Try to use each of the elements in an equally significant way.

   a student, a ramshackle cabin, world domination:

   The school had called a snow day, and Tom had been hunting all day down in the state forest. When he came back to the house, he had no idea where Billy was or what he was up to. He saw the diffuse glow of a single hanging lightbulb coming from the guest cabin located in the far end of the field behind their house. As he brushed through the overgrown reeds in his rubber boots, he saw tiny fireworks bursting sporadically in one of the broken out windows. Billy was doing something with the scraps from the rusted out brick wagon. Tom crept closer. Little glints of light flew, and as Tom felt along the splintery wood walls, it became obvious to him what his brother was doing. The mildewed map of the world was dangling on the wall. The little flags were posted precariously. Billy was at it again.
   — Emily Busch, UM

• In a workshop, assign students (or each other) "titles," based on what you know of students' heritage and inclinations. Titles used in this fashion can send one places one might otherwise not go.

A Convincing Story

One of the powers of a good story is its ability to strengthen an argument. A narrative can be one of the best ways to convince a reader. In essays, in particular, the modes of discourse often get divided—expository, narrative, descriptive writing. But try bringing these elements closer together.

Alice Walker's "Am I Blue" is a good example of a narrative used to make an argument. She tells a story of her experience with a horse, Blue, and how his grief over his mate being removed makes her think about slavery. She looks at the penned horse through the window and likens his life to the experience of her ancestors. Blue is crazed at the loss of his mate and looks so human to Walker's eyes. His grief makes her move through history, through beliefs people have held at different times. She ends her essay with the following words:

> "And it would have to be a white horse, the very image of freedom. And I thought, yes, the animals are forced to become for us merely 'images' of what they once so beautifully expressed. And we are used to drinking milk from containers showing "contented" cows, whose real lives we want to hear nothing about, eating eggs and drumsticks from "happy" hens, and munching hamburgers advertised by bulls of integrity who seem to command their fate. As we talked of freedom and justice one day for all, we sat down to steaks. I am eating misery, I thought, as I took the first bite. And spit it out."

The essay courses through history to arrive at a statement about choices of what we will tolerate, what we will support with our actions. Walker reads the message clearly reflected in Blue's eyes: "Everything you do to us will happen to you; we are your teachers, as you are ours. We are one lesson."

*   *   *

- Think of a story from your life which you might use to create a convincing argument. Try writing the piece as an argumentative essay. Then write your personal story. Which one makes the more compelling argument? You might find that the two join together at some natural point. Perhaps the argument will begin to reveal itself as an extension of the story.

Old Myth, New Myth:
Archetype and the Classics

Our stories never change. They simply take on different forms. Once we learn to recognize archetypes (patterns or models present in the unconscious as well as in our heritage of art), we can often see them at work in sources as varied as fairy tales, nursery rhymes, ancient myths, contemporary stories, and in our own writing. (For discussion of archetypal symbols, see *A Forest of Symbols*. See also *Dream Logic* and "The Jabberwocky" in *Hoppergrass*.)

There are countless sources available today which show how archetypes can be used to understand various aspects of our lives—from psychology, to relationships, to job-related issues. The works of psychologist Carl Jung and mythologist Northrop Frye are classic sources. A rather accessible source as an introduction to archetype is Joseph Campbell. His *Hero with a Thousand Faces* draws on the idea of the same stories existing in different cultures, with the heroes and dragons wearing different faces, but undergoing similar journeys, trials, and revelations. ("The Hero's Adventure," in particular, in a series of videotaped interviews with Campbell called *The Power of Myth,* provides an excellent introduction.)

Of course, there can be a danger in being too aware of archetypes as we re-create them. And one can say this about any kind of art—that, on some level, it is good not to be too aware. Sometimes, the first conscious efforts at using myth or archetype can yield rather clunky results. Nonetheless, it is good practice to let the mind connect story to story, to become familiar with recurring themes, symbols, and sequences of action: the battle, the cycle of life, the forest, the flood, the fountain, the journey, etc. Then they will begin to wander your writing with more fluidity.

All works of art can be explored for archetypal ideas. Certain works themselves have become patterns after which so many other pieces are modeled. Some works declare the influence of such a text in the very title: James Joyce's *Ulysses* or Derek Walcott's *The Odyssey* or *Homeros*, for example, establish the connection with Homer's *Odyssey* and the archetype of the journey.

Many writers use other works of literature, from ancient texts to fairy tales, as explicit points of departure. They might use means such as exploring a particular character or sequence of action, or add an ironic twist or ending. American humorist James Thurber re-tells the story of "Little Red Riding Hood," a classic example of the archetypal encounter in the dark forest. Thurber's version, however, ends with the girl pulling a revolver out of her basket and shooting the wolf dead. The moral which ends the parody is: "Little girls aren't as foolish as they used to be."

Denise Duhamel's and Maureen Seaton's (b.1947) collaborative sonnet sequence, "Madame Bovary" responds to Flaubert's novel, whose central character has become a sort of symbol in our culture. Note how the following excerpt uses modern comparisons for humorous effect, such as the shopping channel and Lotto.

> If anyone ever needed Debtor's
> Anonymous it was Emma Bovary.
> She loved aqua lamp shades and hosiery
> made of pink silk. Her husband was clueless
> re: The big A. Brazen cuckolds slept stress-
> free in Charles' own examining room.
> "Why don't you go shopping with Léon?"
> Charles said, the ultimate dummy in love
> and finance. Thank God no shopping channels
> existed in that part of France. Or Lotto.
> The Medical Convention was not
> where Emma wanted to go for kicks. Paris
> was cruelly tempting with its frivolous
> pastries, its crudités, its Eiffel Tower.

The following poem, "*Memento Mori* in Middle School" recounts a childhood project about *The Inferno*. The poem uses a middle school setting to explore a journey on many levels. Dante himself, in his epic, used a classic archetype of the journey and descent into the dark. The poem offers an interesting example of subject finding form—a loosely-rhymed (exact, slant, assonantal) terza rima in homage to Dante.

DIANE THIEL (b. 1967)

Memento Mori in Middle School

When I was twelve, I chose Dante's Inferno
in gifted class—an oral presentation
with visual aids. My brother, il miglior fabbro,

said he would draw the tortures. We used ten
red posterboards. That day, for school, I dressed
in pilgrim black, left earlier to hang them

around the class. The students were impressed.
The teacher, too. She acted quite amused
and peered too long at all the punishments.

We knew by reputation she was cruel.
The class could see a hint of twisted forms
and asked to be allowed to round the room

as I went through my final presentation.
We passed the first one, full of poets cut
out of a special issue of Horizon.

The class thought these were such a boring set,
they probably deserved their tedious fates.
They liked the next, though—bodies blown about,

the lovers kept outside the tinfoil gates.
We had a new boy in our class named Paolo
and when I noted Paolo's wind-blown state

and pointed out Francesca, people howled.
I knew that more than one of us not-so-
covertly liked him. It seemed like hours

before we moved on to the gluttons, though,
where they could hold the cool fistfuls of slime
I brought from home. An extra touch. It sold

in canisters at toy stores at the time.
The students recognized the River Styx,
the logo of a favorite band of mine.

We moved downriver to the town of Dis,
which someone loudly re-named Dis and Dat.
And for the looming harpies and the furies,

who shrieked and tore things up, I had clipped out
the shrillest, most deserving teacher's heads
from our school paper, then thought better of it.

At the wood of suicides, we quieted.
Though no one in the room would say a word,
I know we couldn't help but think of Fred.

His name was in the news, though we had heard
he might have just been playing with the gun.
We moved on quickly by that huge, dark bird

and rode the flying monster, Geryon,
to reach the counselors, each wicked face,
again, I had resisted pasting in.

To represent the ice in that last place,
where Satan chewed the traitors' frozen heads,
my mother had insisted that I take

an ice-chest full of popsicles—to end
my gruesome project on a lighter note.
"It is a comedy, isn't it," she said.

She hadn't read the poem, or seen our art,
but asked me what had happened to the sweet,
angelic poems I once read and wrote.

The class, though, was delighted by the treat,
and at the last round, they all pushed to choose
their colors quickly, so they wouldn't melt.

The bell rang. Everyone ran out of school,
as always, yelling at the top of their lungs,
The Inferno fast forgotten, but their howls

showed off their darkened red and purple tongues.

*   *   *

• Choose a myth, fairy tale, or other well-known story, and use the general motif or plot to reflect on something or narrate a story (perhaps make it contemporary). You might also change the tale somewhat for comic purposes, as in James Thurber's version of "Little Red Riding Hood," mentioned above. There are numerous models to follow. A few suggestions: Yeats' poem, "Leda and the Swan," Auden's poem, "Musée des Beaux Arts," Anne Sexton's collection of poetry, *Transformations*, Ursula Le Guin's story, "The Wife's Story." If you like, the symbols or patterns of action in the fairy tale or myth might provide more subtle undercurrents for your piece, rather than a re-telling. (Alice Munro's story, "The Found Boat" and Joyce Carol Oates' story "Where Are You Going, Where Have You Been" are a few examples you might use as inspiration.)

• When I use the above exercise with young children, I ask them to write about a character in a nursery rhyme or fairy tale. It can yield unexpected results, such as one second grader, who decided that "Diddle" was a mysterious character in the familiar nursery rhyme.

• Find folk tales or myths from different cultures: Native American, African, Chinese, etc. Note any connections to stories with which you are familiar. Write a piece which explores an archetypal theme or symbol in the stories: creation, a flood, transformation, etc. Perhaps use a line from the tale as an epigraph. (Your response might have a contemporary slant. For instance, write about a flood in your hometown.)

• Respond to a well-known work of literature, perhaps by focusing on a character, or by using modern comparisons for effect, as in *Madame Bovary*. Try emulating the form of the chosen piece in your response, as in the example of *"Memento Mori* in Middle School."

Inhabitation

Robert Frost once wrote, "When I say me in a poem, it's someone else./When I say somebody else, it might be me." Sometimes writing with a different voice allows us to explore aspects about ourselves we might not otherwise reveal. And sometimes it allows us to come closer to someone else's experience. An extension of the previous chapter's exercise might be to inhabit one of the characters in a story (with whom you identify perhaps) and write from the *persona* you create. You could give someone a voice who previously had none. You might also inhabit an animal from a myth or fairy tale. During one workshop, for instance, having asked students to respond to this assignment, I chose to write from the perspective of the lioness, a "character" in Ovid's "Pyramus and Thisbe." Her presence intrigued me—she does not harm either of the lovers, but by her sheer existence, sets in motion the chain of events which leads to their death.

Victorian poet Robert Browning (1812-1889) developed the form of the *dramatic monologue* (a speech which creates a dramatic scene) in a poem. He often used the form to explore the psyches of weak, troubled, or crazy characters. His "My Last Duchess," likely the most famous dramatic monologue ever written, takes on the voice of an Italian Renaissance Duke:

> That's my last Duchess painted on the wall,
> Looking as if she were alive. I call
> That piece a wonder, now; Fra Pandolf's hands
> Worked busily a day, and there she stands...
> ...She thanked men, —good! but thanked
> Somehow—I know not how—as if she ranked
> My gift of a nine-hundred-years-old name
> With anybody's gift.. Who'd stoop to blame...
> ...Oh sir, she smiled, no doubt,
> Whene'er I passed her; but who passed without
> Much the same smile? This grew; I gave commands;
> Then all smiles stopped together. There she stands
> As if alive...

David Malouf's novel, *An Imaginary Life*, assumes the voice of the Roman poet, Ovid, who is exiled to a region where no one can speak his language. It is this element of the story which Malouf enters most fully:

> I have come to a decision. The language I shall teach the Child is the language of these people I have come among, and not after all my own. And in making that decision I know I have made another. I shall never go back to Rome. No doubt I will go on writing to my wife and my attorney. I shall even go on addressing Augustus, begging him to forgive my crimes and recall me. Because in one-half of my life that is what is expected of me, it is the drama I must play out to its conclusion. But in the other half of my life I know that if the letter came, recalling me, I would not go. More and more in these last weeks I have come to realize that this place is the true destination I have been seeking...We barely recognize the annunciation when it comes, declaring: Here is the life you have tried to throw away. Here is your second chance. Here is the destiny you have tried to shake off by inventing a hundred false roles, a hundred false identities for yourself. It will look at first like disaster, but is really good fortune in disguise, since fate too knows how to follow your evasions through a hundred forms of its own. Now you will become at last the one you intended to be.
> — David Malouf (b. 1934)

(See another passage from Malouf in *Natural Tunes.*)

* * *

• Make a list of historical or mythological figures you would like to "inhabit." Consider the particular aspect of their lives which intrigues you. You might need to do some research in order to have your facts straight. Try a dramatic monologue from one of your chosen perspectives, focusing on a particular "story" of his/her life. You may be surprised how the voice comes when you call it.

Inhabitation of Federico Garcia Lorca

People think that being a poet means that every minute there's a poem in your head, that every time of silence, there are little mechanisms in your creative fiber that produce stanzas and lines of love and pain, the only two emotions that are valuable. But it's not that simple. It's not like jumping into a pool and coming out with all sorts of ideas and dreams and stories. Sometimes a poem is written in blood—it comes to you in pain and agony. Sometimes it is like sweet nectar so soothing to the palate...Poetry is fire and ice, my friend.

—Jorge Fernandez, FIU

- Inhabit an animal, or an inanimate object, or natural phenomenon, like a hurricane, perhaps.

Low Pressure Soliloquy

I was born of late summer's dry winds brewed by the great desert in the East. Even then, I was being watched from the heavens. The warm heaving waters brought me strength, and soon I howled in delight. Still without a name, I wandered West without a course, growing in girth and height fed from the ocean's breast. A flying silver bird pierced my eye but would not stay. Now they watched me closer. I made the waves breach the whitecaps. And then the rains began.

Go West, young man —now you'll get a name. As I do my clockwise dance, my millibars fall, and still no landfall. There, far to the East, spins my newborn sister. She follows my path. I hopscotch palmed green islands. There, far to the West, some great landmass will be my journey's end. I'm almost there, but, no, the jet stream from Yukon land blows me back to sea. I spin and bellow to no avail. The New World beckons, but my heart now weakens. Better luck, sister Gerta.

—Fred Sherman, UM

In Character

Dialogue or a character's response to a setting or situation can tell a great deal more about her personality than straight physical description or abstract words. (See, for instance, the excerpt from Connell's *Mrs. Bridge* in *Vignette*.) Another way of revealing character is via the workings of that character's mind. While the earlier novel often contained an omniscient or all-knowing character, many modern novels have no narrator at all. Rather, novelists such as James Joyce and Virginia Woolf bring us into the twists and turns of a character's mind, via a stream-of-consciousness approach. The following passage of Virginia Woolf's *The Waves*, for instance, shows the character, Bernard, in turmoil about writing a letter to the girl he loves. The layers of character development are numerous here, as Bernard admits to creating another persona for the letter:

> "Now, as a proof of my susceptibility to atmosphere, here, as I come into my room, and turn on the light, and see the sheet of paper, the table, my gown lying negligently over the back of the chair, I feel that I am that dashing yet reflective man, that bold and dexterous figure, who, lightly throwing off his cloak, seizes his pen and at once flings off the following letter to the girl with whom he is passionately in love.
>
> "Yes, all is propitious. I am now in the mood. I can write the letter straight off which I have begun ever so many times. I have just come in; I have flung down my hat and my stick; I am writing the first thing that comes into my head without troubling to put the paper straight. It is going to be a brilliant sketch which, she must think, was written without a pause, without an erasure. Look how unformed the letters are—there is a careless blot. All must be sacrificed to speed and carelessness. I will write a quick, running small hand, exaggerating the down stroke of the 'y' and crossing the 't' thus—with a dash. The date shall be only Tuesday, the 17th, and then a question mark. But also I must give her the impression that though he—for this is not myself—is writing in such an offhand, such a slapdash way, there is some subtle suggestion of intimacy and respect. I must allude to talks we have had together—bring back some

remembered scene. But I must seem to her (this is very important) to be passing from thing to thing with the greatest ease in the world. I shall pass from the service for the man who was drowned (I have a phrase for that) to Mrs. Moffat and her sayings (I have a note of them) and so to some reflections apparently casual but full of profundity (profound criticism is often written casually) about some book I have been reading, some out-of-the-way book. I want her to say as she brushes her hair or puts out the candle, 'Where did I read that? Oh, in Bernard's letter.' It is the speed, the hot, molten effect, the lava flow of sentence into sentence that I need. Who am I thinking of? Byron, of course. I am, in some ways, like Byron. Perhaps a sip of Byron will help to put me in the vein. Let me read a page. No; this is dull; this is scrappy. This is rather too formal. Now I am getting the hang of it. Now I am getting his beat into my brain (the rhythm is the main thing in writing). Now, without pausing I will begin, on the very lilt of the stroke —

"Yet it falls flat. It peters out. I cannot get up steam enough to carry me over the transition. My true self breaks off from my assumed. And if I begin to rewrite it, she will feel, 'Bernard is posing as a literary man; Bernard is thinking of his biographer' (which is true). No, I will write the letter tomorrow directly after breakfast."

—Virginia Woolf (1882-1941)

* * *

- Write a description of a character's physical qualities, using details such as bumping one's head on the doorway or wearing shoe-lifts, or causing a stir when he or she walks into the room.

- Use dialogue or a sequence of action to reveal a character's personality.

- Freewriting, in effect, reveals our own stream-of-consciousness. Try getting "in character," and freewriting as that character, in order to create the mental wanderings of the character's mind. (One caution: Go deeply into your character, but leave more than a trail of bread crumbs to find your way back.)

Tapping the Trickster

Cultures all over the world have trickster figures. Coyote is the most well-known in North America, while Spider is most common to West Africa. Fox and Raven figure in many South American cultures, and the familiar god Loki figures as the trickster figure of Norse mythology.

The trickster is generally heroic, but also cunning and deceptive. He is definitely a figure of duality. All of us have a little trickster in us, which social conventions often keep from surfacing. Writers tend to be more likely to allow the trickster to appear, perhaps because writing involves a kind of seduction of the reader.

As children, we are all told not to lie, and yet, in truth, much of our lives we end up telling lies: tiny harmless "white" lies, perhaps, but lies nonetheless. In telling "white" lies, though, we often deny our true selves. In writing, on the other hand, we can tell huge lies. We can invent personas, embody our dreams, tell the tallest of tales. In fact, the taller they are, sometimes, the more true they become. We can reveal much of our true selves when we invent personas through which to speak, or create metaphor. It could be said that all metaphor is, in a sense, a lie, because it presents one thing as something else. And yet it so often has the effect of getting closer to the truth.

* * *

• The following exercise is a good one to access the true events of our lives which are strange enough to sound like lies. Write three short statements or anecdotes about yourself—two lies and one truth, with the same level of believability. In a workshop, it can be fun to have a few volunteers read their responses, and let others guess which is the truth.

1. When I was born, I was two months premature and kept in an incubator on life support. I grew rapidly, to the surprise of the medical professionals.

2. In the summer of 1995, my father discharged a firearm at me as I sat demurely in my treehouse overlooking the main house. He said it was an accident, but never really apologized. (truth)

3. In sixth grade, I got lost in New York City and ended up being escorted back to the police station through Central Park, on horseback.
—Jen Pearson, UM

• Tell an absolute lie which somehow is true to the way you feel.

Today, as my Spanish teacher began to speak, there was a loud sound like an explosion, and she just vanished. We waited for a couple of minutes, and then we all came to the conclusion that she wasn't coming back.
—Emily Busch, UM

The initial results of these exercises are frequently the seeds of longer pieces.

History, Herstory

Researching history can be a way to access the past and connect it to the present and the future. But the research has to mean something. It has to become personal. "History is your own heartbeat," as Michael Harper says. In the following poem, "American History," Harper addresses the invisibility of African Americans in American culture. The title, compression, and juxtaposition of events suggest the great gaps in standard accounts of history.

MICHAEL HARPER (b. 1938)

American History

Those four black girls blown up
in that Alabama church
remind me of five hundred
middle passage blacks,
in a net, under water
in Charleston harbor
so redcoats wouldn't find them.
Can't find what you can't see
can you?

History has varying accounts, depending on the speaker. James Loewen's *Lies My Teacher Told Me* is a great source of alternative perspectives on American history. A few chapter titles give a sense of the contents: "The Truth about the First Thanksgiving," "The Invisibility of Racism in American History Textbooks," "Progress is our Most Important Product." Howard Zinn's *A People's History of the United States* is another such source.

Giving an ancestor a voice which she or he might not have had otherwise can be an empowering act. It also makes history more personal. Alice Walker's essay, "In Search of Our Mother's Gardens," speaks about the creative spirit which found its way into quilts and gardens, but which also traveled down the lineage. We are their voices:

And so our mothers and grandmothers have, more often than not anonymously, handed on the creative spark, the seed of the flower they themselves never hoped to see: or like a sealed letter they could not plainly read.
— Alice Walker (b. 1944)

*   *   *

- Choose an ancestor who has always interested you, and do some research on events which took place during his or her life.

- Do some personal research. "Interview" your family members about family history. Record what you hear. You may find that the story you are seeking has always been at your fingertips.

- Start with a single incident. It might be hard to get started if you think you have to tell a whole life story. So just start with one story—perhaps one the family still tells, the one which survived via the oral tradition.

- Write a story from the perspective of an ancestor. Try to inhabit his or her experience. (See *Inhabitation*.)

- Narrate a historical event either from the perspective of a participant or an observer, as in the following evocative poem:

ENID SHOMER (b. 1944)

Women Bathing at Bergen-Belsen

April 24, 1945

Twelve hours after the Allies arrive
there is hot water, soap. Two women bathe
in a makeshift, open-air shower while nearby
fifteen thousand are flung naked into mass graves
by captured SS guards. Clearly legs and arms
are the natural handles of a corpse. The bathers,

taken late in the war, still have flesh
on their bones, still have breasts. Though nudity was
a death sentence here, they have undressed,
oblivious to the soldiers and the cameras.
The corpses push through the limed earth like upended
headstones. The bathers scrub their feet, bending
in beautiful curves, mapping the contours
of the body, that kingdom to which they've returned.

A Click of Closure

Robert Frost says, "Anyone can get into a poem. It takes a poet to get out of one." W.B. Yeats believed good closure occurred when a poem would "come shut with a click, like a closing box." What gives a piece of writing that click? It is hard to identify, but we know it when we see or hear it. Evan Connell's vignettes both shut like a door at the end, and yet also echo into the next chapter. (See *Vignettes.*) This is the quality closure should have—it should reverberate.

A poignant or startling image or moment can make for good closure, in prose or poetry. Alice Walker's example in her narrative essay "Am I Blue," for instance, ends with the speaker spitting out "misery." (See *A Convincing Story.*) Likewise, the poem, "*Memento Mori* in Middle School," closes with the image of the children yelling after school, showing off "their darkened red and purple tongues." (See *Old Myth, New Myth.*)

Closure is sometimes influenced by form. Sonnets, for instance, traditionally closed with a philosophical commentary. And several poetic forms, such as the villanelle, have refrains which often carry a slightly different meaning in the end. (See Elizabeth Bishop's "One Art" in *Villanelle.*) A piece might also be left mysterious. Walter de la Mare's "The Listeners," is ambiguous, leaving the reader to imagine the precise events. (See *Ballads and Ballades.*)

Some writers favor the ironic ending, which usually has to be set up from the beginning. The irony of Ursula LeGuin's vignette, "The Wife's Story," for instance, becomes clear close to the end of the story, as it becomes apparent that the speaker is a wolf. In Alice Munro's "How I Met My Husband," the title and first twelve pages prepare you for one kind of story, as they describe how the speaker met and fell in love with a dashing air show pilot. However, a radical shift occurs in the last two paragraphs. Edie, the main character, has been waiting for a promised letter from her first love, going down daily to meet the mail:

Till it came to me one day there were women doing this with their lives, all over. There were women just waiting and waiting by mailboxes for one letter or another. I imagined me making this journey day after day and year after year, and my hair starting to get gray...So I stopped meeting the mail...

I was surprised when the mailman phoned the Peebles' place in the evening and asked for me. He said he missed me. He asked if I would like to go to Goderich, where some well-known movie was on, I forget now what. So I said yes, and I went out with him for two years and he asked me to marry him, and we were engaged a year more while I got my things together, and then we did marry. He always tells the children the story of how I went after him by sitting by the mailbox every day, and naturally I laugh and let him, because I like for people to think what pleases them and makes them happy.
—Alice Munro (b. 1931)

Poems also often carry an element of surprise at the end. Dorothy Parker's poems, for instance, are known for their ironic twists, such as, "One Perfect Rose," which is set up as a love poem, with a refrain of "one perfect rose" that the speaker's love always brings. The twist comes in the last stanza, when the speaker wonders why her love has never sent her yet, "one perfect limousine, do you suppose?" Consider, also, the effect of the closure in the following poem:

EDWIN ARLINGTON ROBINSON (1869-1935)

Richard Cory

Whenever Richard Cory went down town,
We people on the pavement looked at him:
He was a gentleman from sole to crown,
Clean favored, and imperially slim.

And he was always quietly arrayed,
And he was always human when he talked;
But he still fluttered pulses when he said,
"Good morning," and he glittered when he walked.

And he was rich—yes, richer than a king—
And admirably schooled in every grace:
In fine, we thought that he was everything
To make us wish that we were in his place.

So on we worked, and waited for the light,
And went without the meat, and cursed the bread;
And Richard Cory, one calm summer night,
Went home and put a bullet through his head.

In the case of "Richard Cory," the end of the poem "makes" the poem, because it is unexpected. The ending works not just because of the element of surprise, but because it reflects accurately the way such events feel when they occur.

There is an old German proverb regarding closure: "Beginning and end shake hands with each other." Sometimes we know when we have reached the end, and it happens naturally, perhaps with an organic, circular structure which contains elements of the opening. Other times we have an idea, but it takes a while to find the right words. And sometimes a piece does not seem to find an end. Try not to force it. It might be telling you to continue down that road.

*   *   *

• Exchange your writing. Rather often, workshops tend to address the effectiveness of the closure, and often a natural closure already exists. Sometimes, we don't know when to stop.

• Try writing a piece with an ironic closure. Play the trickster. Some real-life stories have a natural irony when they occur, with a clear closure, a line of dialogue, perhaps.

Drawing the Circle

We may not usually think of storytelling as a communal activity, but our stories have many different voices telling them simultaneously, with many versions and perspectives. There can be great power in the "telling," just as there is another strength in knowing when to be silent, and listen. It helps to think of writing as communal, particularly in the often jarring rhythms of our competitive world. Some years ago, during a difficult stretch, a close friend sent me a small note which said, "Just because the field is competitive, doesn't mean you have to be." It was something I needed to hear at the time. Lessons sometimes arrive when we are ready to accept them—via books, poems, people. I put the note in my window like a talisman, where it remains today. Striving for beauty and wholeness in our life-work is not a race to the finish. It helped me to keep this in mind, to keep things in perspective, to continue working.

There is another quotation in my window which reaches out to me here:

> Love and the imminence of love and intolerable remembering,
> Dreams like buried treasure, generous luck,
> And memory itself, where a glance can make you dizzy—
> All this was given to you and with it
> The ancient nourishment of heroes—
> Treachery, defeat, humiliation.
> —Jorge Luis Borges (1899-1986)

It can be helpful, albeit difficult over the years, to think of even the defeat and treachery we encounter as blessings, as nourishment. Our setbacks are part of the weave of the story, sometimes to realign us with our true directions.

Building a community, a circle of people you trust and with whom you feel safe sharing your stories, your defeats, and your triumphs is a vital part of being a writer. Shared experience is a source of energy to open new perspectives and possibilities. Recognizing the communal nature of storytelling is a way to truly connect with each other and with our world—to use our gifts, reclaim our natural rhythms, find equilibrium and balance.

*   *   *

- Early in this book, I suggest reclaiming our oral traditions by learning and sharing poems by heart. It is one of the most powerful ways to tap into your individual and cultural memories and discover your rhythm. Create a circle for voices to be heard.

- Use the Native American tradition of a story circle to create a communal story or poem. Have one person begin a narrative and speak for two or three minutes. The next person continues the story and so on, until everyone has had a chance to contribute (perhaps twice). When we share any responses in a circle, it can be inspiring to hear the weave of different voices, each lovely and distinct, but part of a greater whole. We can use such story circles to find and create community. We are all part of an ongoing story.

Acknowledgments

Bishop, Elizabeth. "One Art" from *The Complete Poems: 1927-1979*, by Elizabeth Bishop. Copyright 1979, 1983 by Alice Helen Methfessel. Reprinted by permission of Farrar, Straus, and Giroux, LLC.

Bly, Robert. "Cricket," translation of *Issa*. Reprinted by permission of the poet.

Cambridge, Gerry. "Goldfinch in Spring" from *The Shell House*, Scottish Cultural Press, 1995. Reprinted by permission of the poet.

Cope, Wendy. "Lonely Hearts" from *Making Cocoa for Kingsley Amis*, 1986. Reprinted by permission of Faber and Faber Ltd.

Cunningham, J.V. "I Drive Westward" from *The Collected Poems & Epigrams of J.V. Cunningham*, Ohio University Press/Swallow Press, Athens,1971. Reprinted by permission of Ohio University Press/Swallow Press.

Davis, Dick. "I Hide Within my Poems as I Write Them" from *Borrowed Ware*, Mage Publishers, 1997. Reprinted by permission of the poet.

Duhamel, Denise and Seaton, Maureen. "Madame Bovary." Reprinted by permission of the poets.

Espaillat, Rhina. "Bilingual/Bilingue" from *Where Horizons Go*, New Odyssey Press, 1998. Reprinted by permission of the poet.

Finch, Annie. "Sapphics for Patience" from *Eve*, Story Line Press, 1997. Reprinted by permission of the poet.

Gioia, Dana. "My Confessional Sestina" from *The Gods of Winter*, Graywolf Press. Copyright 1991 by Dana Gioia. Reprinted by permission of Graywolf Press, Saint Paul, Minnesota.

Shomer, Enid. "Women Bathing at Bergen Belsen" from *Stalking the Florida Panther*, The Word Works,1987. Copyright 1985 by Enid Shomer. Reprinted by permission of the poet.

Simpson, Louis. "American Poetry" from *A Poetry Collection*. Reprinted by permission of the author and Story Line Press.

Whitlow, Carolyn Beard. "Rockin" a Man Stone Blind" from *Wild Meat*, Lost Road Press, 1986. Reprinted by permission of the poet.